How Business Started

Also by PETER SEIDLER

Handbuch Industrieböden (Industrial Floors Handbook)

Kunststoffe auf der Baustelle (Polymers On-Site)

RILEM State-of-the-Art Report *Industrial Floors*

Congress Proceedings / Tagungshandbücher
International Colloquia *Industrial Floors* 1987–2007

How Business Started
On Freedom, Law and Liberal-Mindedness

Three Essays on Economic History and Entrepreneurship by Peter Seidler

German edition:
Wie das Wirtschaften begann
Über Freiheit, Recht und Weltoffenheit
Drei Essays zur Wirtschaftsgeschichte
Bibliographic information published by
Die Deutsche Nationalbibliothek:
Die Deutsche Nationalbibliothek lists this publication
in the Deutsche Nationalbibliografie;
detailed bibliographic data are available on the Internet at
http://dnb.d-nb.de

English edition
Translation by Books on Demand GmbH, Norderstedt [jk]
© 2010 by Peter Seidler (German edition)
© 2013 by Peter Seidler (English edition)

Cover illustration: "God, the Builder of the Universe" (about
1050) – *Source:*
British Library – publication by D. Hägermann *Technik im
frühen Mittelalter zwischen 500 und 1000*, in W. König (ed.): *Propyläen
Technikgeschichte*, Vol. 1, p. 331, Berlin 1991

Typography and cover design,
printed and published by:
BoD – Books on Demand
ISBN: 978-3-8482-7442-0

Preliminary remarks

Part I: Liberalism in the economy around 1250
How free were the High Middle Ages?
European monasteries and cities outside the feudal system

Part II: Legal certainty and prosperity

Part III: An opening up to the world around 1000
Catalonia between Christianity and Islam

For Christa

About the three essays: Freedom, Law and Liberal-Mindedness

These essays are the result of my research into the origins of economic thought as part of a course in *Philosophy of Economics* at the FernUniversität Hagen. In this connection, I adopted a somewhat glib and occasionally polemical approach to the undertaking in an attempt to alleviate any boredom. Due to the wealth of collated material, it was sometimes necessary to abridge certain sections aphoristically, which means that the essays require further in-depth study involving the critical perusal of the sources and comparison with the huge amount of secondary literature As this would take the essays far beyond the scope, however, I decided to dispense with this task. In embarking on this venture, I found out more about the role that economic action – in which I have taken an active part since 1963 – plays in contributing to a society's prosperity. I was particularly moved by a number of questions. It has not been possible, however, to provide a comprehensive answer – and certainly not a universally valid one – in this context, but only one based on my own experience. They are:

- Why property? What are the historic origins?
- Skills and emancipation of individuals
- Behaviour and organisation of groups
  - Group heterogeneity: rules for action
  - Self-organisation vs. chaos
  - Binding regulations (natural vs. statute laws)
- Can socialism work? If so, how?

"*The Ethical Foundations of Economics*" (1993) by J. J. Piderit, a former President of the Loyola University in Chicago, came to my aid in that respect. Like the Catholic Social Doctrine, it lays down simple principles – based on the tradition of the Bible – that translate into guidelines for action. These include the principles of **efficiency** and **subsidiarity**, whose considerable significance is often underestimated. Coupled with the principles of **liberty** and technical **progress**, their implementation can lead to great prosperity, which then helps to solve the social problem of underprivileged minorities through self-help.

The word 'social' might even be omitted, as F. A. Hayek suggests in "The Fatal Conceit – The Errors of Socialism" (1988) in a chapter on "Our Poisoned Language". According to him this is a weasel word and *has probably become the most confusing expression in our entire moral and political vocabulary* (p. 114) citing Confucius: "*When words lose there meaning, people will lose their liberty*". There is also a section dealing with A. MacIntyre and his affinity with Aristotle's world view in *"After virtue"* (1981). J. Habermas' interview with a number of Christians on the subject of "Devoutness of thought" really impressed me[1]. C. Geyer wrote a report on it and raised the question[2]: "*Is not every edifice of thought, no matter how rigidly it has been composed, built on the sand of our respective moods?*"

*'If there's no meaning in it', said the King,
'that saves a world of trouble, you know,
as we needn't try to find any.'*

Lewis Carroll: Alice's Adventures in Wonderland
(1865)

Part I:
Liberalism in the economy around 1250

*How free were the High Middle Ages?
European monasteries and cities outside the feudal system*

Abstract

This essay focuses on "Liberalism in the economy around 1250 – how free were the High Middle Ages? European monasteries and cities outside the feudal system" by way of an introduction to the subject matter and for discussion purposes.

This section of the paper is divided into two parts: "The state of Europe in the Middle Ages" and "Ethics: Freedom and serfdom" [4]. It raises the question as to the intellectual and economic conditions that must have existed in the Middle Ages between 1000 and 1350 to allow the first industrial revolution to take place. I should point out that some authors refer to the period around 1250 as the start of the Renaissance. The technical advancement that initially took hold in the Cistercian monasteries, in particular, and then led to the construction of the mighty cathedrals, played a key role in this development. It was, however, only able to flourish outside feudalism in the freedom and liberal anarchy that often prevailed, along with relatively dependable legal certainty and uninterrupted by the balance of power, in the monasteries and cities.

Many universities also enjoyed a limited form of freedom, and it was there that innovations pushed technical and scientific advancement forward. In this connection, I would like to name Thomas Aquinas (1225–1274), the philosopher and theologian, as one of the earliest and most influential teachers of the time. Together with the principles of efficiency and subsidiarity, the tenets of the Catholic Social Doctrine, which were not laid down in writing until much later, are likely to have contributed to this development. It was the clergy's change in attitude to monetary matters that paved the way for the revolution in trade and triggered the zeitgeist for reform.

The idea that individualism linked to liberalism was able to exist at all in medieval times is frequently challenged. The following excerpt from a letter written by the notable Doctor of the church, Bernard of Clairvaux (1091–1153) to his disciple Pope Eugenius should serve as proof of the existence of individualism:

> *Give yourself some space! I'm not saying: Do it all the time. But I am saying: Keep on doing it, again and again. Be there for yourself, in the same way that you are available to everyone else.*

TABLE OF CONTENTS

Preliminary remarks

R. Metz sums up his history of German economics in his pronouncements on "secular trends" on a highly sceptical note without even expanding on the problematic aspects alluded to in his observations:

"At the end of our century, the belief in technological advancement (…) has given way to a more sceptical view. It is no longer possible to simply equate technological evolution with progress, modernisation and a higher standard of living."

I detect a certain pessimism that is not justified by anything but leads straight to the defeatism of Oswald Spengler's "The Decline of the West" (1918), and thus directly to irrationalism. Provided we look to the right institutions, common sense is capable of dealing with existing problems. It is up to the universities to ensure that this conviction becomes more widespread. So the decision of the FernUniversität Hagen to offer a course in "Philosophy of Economics" was highly welcome. I would like to take this opportunity to commit a few thoughts to paper, even though they require further refinement and research. It seems to me, however, that only liberalism, as formulated by the Nobel laureate Hayek but within the limits outlined by Kant, Buchanan, Rawls, Nell-Breuning, Piderit, etc., is capable of solving our problems. One thing needs to be borne in mind, though: evolution is not, and has never necessarily been, of benefit to the weakest in society. Where the weak are given too much protection in a democratic economy, the talented individuals needed to boost the country's economic and technical progress often look elsewhere, and this triggers the "brain drain" and decline happening in Europe right now.

We are fortunate in that we are familiar with the misguided efforts that were repeatedly supported by irrational philosophers: the Inquisition with its crusades, Counter-Enlightenment, communism, Marxism and all kinds of fascism. In a word: intolerance. Not only the occurrences in Toledo in 1492, which was, after all, the year in which America was rediscovered, but also the Sicilian Vespers, the destruction of the Cathars and the Templars, the St. Bartholomew's Day massacre, the burning of Giordano Bruno or the execution of Lavoisier should give us something to think about. What is called for is the emancipation of the citizens – not some contrived diktats of government. How does the role of the Christian church, which is a church for the weak yet which once openly belonged to the opponents of the Enlightenment, need to develop? How do other religions have to change? Why is this fundamental problem not discussed more widely with a view to inducing change before it is too late? Or, to emulate Kant: What can be done to reduce the *lack of emancipation*? What can be done about immature, unemancipated individuals? In this sense, my essay should be regarded as a beginning.

1. On the situation in Europe in the Middle Ages

1.1 The year 1000

It was in 2000 that I reread the doctoral thesis written by José Ortega y Gasset at the age of 21 on "The Terrors of the Year One Thousand". I was trying to find out what I might use for the economic history of the 11th and 12th centuries, which were of interest to me in this context in my research into an earlier form of "liberalism". The supposed terrors put a tremendous strain on economic development. I am fascinated by the wealth of details; they show how, one thousand years ago, the church elevated ignorance to an end in itself, leading to a situation in which human beings were apparently unable to evolve further. The church hindered the emergence of new ideas, wherever it could. Education and formal training were reserved for a privileged few. The remainder of the population were deprived of knowledge. But no revelations have ever come out of ignorance … Here are a few excerpts from the aforementioned thesis, which I have arranged under headings for the sake of clarity.

Millennium
"So the terrors of the year 1000 are untrue …"

Confusion
"Institutions, feelings, beliefs, economic activity, learning, everything is in a state of confusion, at the beginning of its development …"

Serfdom
"Bear this principle in mind: 'He who loves my hen is my rooster'. So you are part of my chicken farm. Lay down your sword. From this day on, you are my bondsman."

Revolt of the masses
"In 997 the peasants in Normandy joined forces in an attempt to overthrow their masters."

A fief in lieu of ownership by purchase
"The legal basis at the time (…) was the fief [feudum], or gift of land, just as it was ownership through purchase under ancient Roman law."

Hierarchy
"… rank was even taken into account in the choice of wet nurse; the son of a king had to be suckled by a duchess, the son of a duke by a countess, etc."

Rights
"… and we won't say anything more about holding sway over life and death, because even fairly unimportant baronies possessed this right."

Power of St. Benedict
"Hugo Capet's last words were addressed to Robert (his successor): '(…) and make quite sure that you don't arouse the anger of the patriarch of the monasteries, the great St. Benedict'."

Literacy and documents
"After all, there were hardly any notaries so documents were agreed orally and verified by the Bishop some time later."

Disregard for knowledge
"… since Fulco (the Good, Count of Anjou) had noticed the disdain the King (Louis, the German) had shown for his knowledge, he wrote him these proud words: 'You should be aware, Sire, that an illiterate king is like a crowned donkey.'"

Scientists as conjurers
"… when people saw how Gerbert and Abbo revolutionised geometry (…) they regarded them both as conjurers who could only have acquired such wonderful knowledge by signing a pact with the devil."

Cluny prohibits thought
"Cluny gradually gained ground, but it overdid its austerity; it was merciless in its treatment of human nature, 'denying it all forms of pleasure, even those of the mind'."

Poor state of knowledge
"Academic knowledge was pitiful and extremely weak during these centuries …"

Centred on the salvation of one's soul
"The monastic schools focused mainly or almost exclusively on religious topics. The teachers paid hardly any attention to the sciences, and classical antiquity was forbidden for dogmatic reasons."

Unnecessary burning of books
"When Odo took 100 books to the Basel community, there was not a single profane tome among them."

Knowledge is rationed

"Just like Cluny, Gorze monastery also dismissed studying the ancient world."

It was in 1904 – over 100 years ago – that Ortega y Gasset employed these words in his description of the wretched world in which he and his academic jurors imaged people lived at the turn of the century, with a high rate of infant mortality, epidemics and famine.

If the following section is largely restricted to Germany, this is due to the sources at my disposal, particularly the history of German economics over the course of a millennium: "Deutsche Wirtschaftsgeschichte – ein Jahrtausend im Überblick" (German Economic History) edited by Michael North. But I have also endeavoured to draw parallels with Germany from other sources, because Europe was essentially a common economic market at that time, with Latin as the "lingua franca".

In the year 700, fewer than one million people lived in the richly forested region now occupied by Germany, each of whom had, on average, 400,000 m² of land at their disposal. In other words, Germany was very sparsely populated. Between the onset of the medieval industrial revolution and about 1350, the population grew to 14 million, with the equivalent of 20,000 m² of land per person. Now, there is only an average of about 3,000 m² for each of today's 80 million Germans. What were the underlying causes for the population's 14-fold increase within the space of 550 years? What was the economic basis?

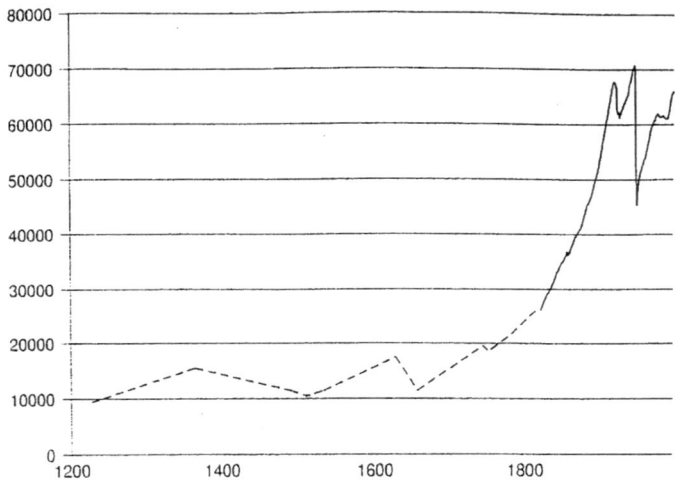

Fig. 1: Population growth in Germany from 1200–1995[3]
(in thousands)

It started off as a subsistence economy: people had just enough to avoid starvation. How could they handle change?

What led to the tremendous economic boom at the time of the Gothic cathedrals? It is true that the first cathedral was built by Father Suger in Saint-Denis in just 15 years, from 1130 to 1144? Where did the money come from?

There are lots of questions to be answered before a person can understand that technical and economic progress were seen by the majority as a valuable asset.

23

1.2 Feudalism

What is feudalism?

As a form of political organisation, feudalism broadly refers to the division and, consequently, the devolution of authority. Landowners living in castles or manors held political sway but were subservient to the lords in their role as vassals, although they retained their economic and social autonomy. Possession of the land extended to ownership of the peasants. Ortega wrote:

"The State boundaries are changing almost every day, the vassal's obligations to the lord increase or decrease without warning; there is one ruler today, and tomorrow you have to obey a different one; and it is not unheard of that someone goes to bed as a free man and wakes up as a bondsman."[4]

This system of society had fully established itself in rural Europe between the 10th and 14th centuries. There were nevertheless tentative signs of a certain liberalism. Legal certainty was, however, often less than assured and there was nothing anyone could do but wait and see[5].

Why leave feudalism behind?

The principle of subsidiarity may be admirably developed in a feudal system, because even the power over life and death, from the emperor to the king and from the king to the baron, is resolutely delegated rather than distributed. But, in spite of the church, this kind of system is lacking in what we regard as fundamental human rights and, as it seems, can only be asserted if power is split between the law, legislation and executive action with the backing of a strong constitution. The landowner has free, unpredictable control over the lives of his bondsmen, without being answerable to his lord. Goethe describes this state of affairs very vividly in his version of the medieval epic "Reynard the Fox".

In the ruler's own personal interest, it is unlikely that he would have used his power to the detriment of the people entrusted to his care. But if an individual's right to freedom and personal development represents a constitutional or human right, there must have been resistance under feudal rule whenever the conduct of the lord was perceived as unjust or a supply crisis arose.

Some people inevitably acquired some sort of education, despite the very limited means of communication, and then realised that their "bondage" could never be a Christian natural law, even though the church was always on the side of the State authority and tried to persuade the people that they should abide by the will of the lord of the manor in all matters. There were human responsibilities (Küng) but no human rights. It was possible to attain a level of relative freedom in monasteries and cities, although the power of the abbots and aldermen should not be underestimated.

Needless to say, every aspect of personal liberty was restricted by the limits imposed by intelligence, state of knowledge and, above all, financial means. This still applies today, 200 years after Kant and the French Revolution which, thanks to the Enlightenment, swept away the Ancien Regime. Not even the aberrations of socialism and the theories of social justice regarding the distribution of available riches make any difference. Kant made several noteworthy observations on a person's self-inflicted lack of emancipation, which I would like to quote, as follows:

"... It is so convenient to be immature! If I have a book to have understanding in place of me, a spiritual adviser to have a conscience for me, a doctor to judge my diet for me, and so on, I need not make any efforts at all. I need not think, so long as I can pay; others will soon enough take the tiresome job over for me ..." [6]

Fortunately, there were always people who queried established knowledge, gained new insights and implemented them, too. According to Kant, it is not surprising that these innovators met with hefty resistance. The burning of Giordano Bruno by the Curia 400 years ago, on 17 February 1600, at the Campo de' Fiori in the centre of Rome is one proof of intellectual intolerance and should be engraved in man's collective memory.

The State and the power vacuum

Occasionally a power vacuum arose, when authority lapsed, which was apparently the reason why part of the population lived in a state of anarchy in the Middle Ages which, according to J. Buchanan, was certainly better than being ruled by a despotic tyrant, living in a feudal society or under a fascist or Marxist totalitarian regime. Since legal certainty was extremely precarious, however, hardly any headway was made in the interregnum period between the fall of the Roman

Empire around 500 A.D., the brief recovery during the reign of King Charlemagne around 800 A.D. and the height of the Middle Ages around 1200, which a minority regard as the beginning of the Renaissance. This long-awaited progress only took off with the flourishing of the monasteries, particularly the Cistercian orders under Bernard of Clairvaux, who was of noble birth, and then – likewise based on their economic activity – the independent cities.

Fig. 2: The most important Cistercian abbeys and their daughter houses[7] (according to Duby 1991)

J. Le Goff identifies the emergence of two new social classes during this period: (1) the merchant bankers and (2) the intellectuals, who both displayed the ability to create something new in an era that was basically opposed to every form of innovation. In "The Road to Serfdom", F. Hayek shows how socialism inevitably leads back in the opposite direction, i.e. to servitude or slavery. The truth of these words became abundantly clear in the Marxist Empire prior to its collapse. The memoirs of the Russian inventor of the hydrogen bomb, A. Sacharow, who later played an active role in the peace movement, are an eloquent documentation. F. Crouzet expresses this clearly, too, referring to D. L. Landes with regard to the technical advancement achieved with artistically embellished watch movements:

"Around 1300 – following three particularly creative centuries in terms of practical matters without any interference from virtually non-existent states – Europe was densely populated, mobile, active and dynamic. Literacy, schooling, writing and arithmetic had made a remarkable recovery. New mentalities – which were not 'medieval' in the usual sense of the word – were emerging. The demand for precise bookkeeping had developed in trading circles from the end of the 12th century onwards. The introduction of Arabic numerals considerably simplified accounting, calculating and measuring practice." [8]

In more recent years, M. Brater and C. Munz have pointed out the educational effects of bookkeeping.[9] The monetary system had, moreover, developed sufficiently since the end of the 11th century so trade was now much easier.[10] In view of the numerous other innovations – including non-metallic currency – M. Bloch even spoke of a "monetary revolution".[11]

Legal certainty on journeys

It was possible to achieve a degree of legal certainty within the walls of monasteries and cities.[12] But, as Marco Polo wrote in 1298, travelling from Venice to Peking was usually safe, too, because the ruling powers had joined forces against the highwaymen and pirates. Nothing was to stand in the way of trade and change if the entire population, including the rulers, were not to descend into poverty. It is thanks not only to him but also to the great Arabian travellers Ibn Fadlan (around 900), Ibn Jubayr (around 1200) and Ibn Battuta (around 1350) that we know so much about the state of the world outside Europe during the Middle Ages, which were not so dark, after all.[13]

Tolerant, intelligent individuals were called upon to solve transcultural ethical conflicts[14] like the coexistence of people of different faiths in Toledo until the expulsion of the Jews in 1492 – the year in which America was rediscovered, incidentally – or as Lessing described in "Nathan the Wise".

More recently, the freedom of travel led to the enormous wave of skilled, intelligent Europeans emigrating to North America, where human rights were written down in the Constitution even before the French Revolution and – to emulate P. Sloterdijk – where the Roman Empire was transferred following the latest Thirty Years' War (1914 – 1945)[15]. This goes so far that we can read the following view in an article published by the sociologist A. Schuller:

"The multipolar world order is a threat to peace. The United States should become the hegemony of mankind."[16]

1.3 What's the point of economic action?

First of all, we have to clarify why we should engage in economic activity at all. Economics is one of several academic disciplines that deal with this topic. The following definition is to be found in P. A. Samuelson and D. Nordhaus:

"Economics is the study of how people and society end up choosing, with or without the use of money, to employ scarce productive resources that could have alternative uses to produce various commodities over time and distributing them for consumption, now or in the future, among various persons or groups in society. (It analyses costs and benefits of improving patterns of resource allocation.)"[17]

Economics essentially deals with the phenomenon of work efficiency and its organisation. Industrial sociology has shed light on it by means of systematic field analysis. Aristotle also gave thought to "economic affairs", and we should not omit Xenophon's "Oeconomicus".[18] An Arabian/North African definition of the term "work" by the "Father of Sociology"[19] Ibn Khaldun (1332–1406), i.e. at the end of the 700-year political hegemony of the Arabs, is of particular interest. He wrote as follows[20]:

"Human labour is necessary for every profit and capital accumulation. When (the source of profit) is work, it is obvious. When the source of gain is animal, plants, or minerals, human labour is still necessary. Without it, no gain will be obtained (…) (Man) obtains (some profit) through no efforts of his own, as, for instance, through rain that makes the fields thrive, and similar things. But resources are only a contributory element; human

effort (labour) must be combined with them for wealth creation. That there must be a share of labour in profit is obvious. (…) It should be further known that the capital a person earns and acquires, if resulting from a craft, is the value realized from his labour. Some crafts are partly associated with other crafts. For example, carpentry and weaving are associated with wood and yarn respectively for production. However, the labour that goes into the production processes is more important and its value is higher. If profit results from something other than a craft, the value of that profit and of the capital acquired from it is the contribution of the labour spent in obtaining them. (…) It has, thus, become clear that gains and profits in their entirety or for most part, are value realized from human labour."

This view was presumably widespread around 1200, and earlier. Usurious interest and profiteering, prohibited on pain of punishment by the church until well into the 12th century, are a different problem.

1.4 Natural sciences: "falsification"

The systematic exploration of the laws of nature was another aspect. Roger Bacon (ca 1220–1292) evidently succeeded in inventing gunpowder – a discovery that was to change the world forever – parallel to, but independent of its early development in China and the almost simultaneous one in Germany.

Scientific curiosity and the fun of hypothetical questions were the prerequisites for secular inventions of this kind – as well as for the construction of cathedrals, for example – meaning that the human mind thought up all sorts of things in order to use their subsequent realisation to improve people's standards of living. The practical implementation of an idea led to new hypotheses which, in turn, were put to the test: the dawn of empirical analysis.

Yet this also entailed the "falsification" of ideas, as K. Popper referred to this process in later years. The "falsification", coupled with the procedure adopted by the academics, went on to play an important role in scientific theory according to Kuhn, Lakatos, Newton-Smith and Johnson-Laird, to name just a few. What is often forgotten, however, as R. Dunbar points out, is that the original concept of "falsification" goes back much earlier and should be attributed to Aristotle (De Caelo)[21].

"Whenever one lights upon more exact proofs, then we must be grateful to the discoverer, but for the present we must state what seems plausible."

Or in 1653 – 300 years before K. Popper – in W. Harvey's "On the Generation of Animals" (De Generatione Animalium)[22]:

"I only ask as my just deserts the liberty I freely allow to all other men, to put forward as true those things which in this whole dark business seem probable until such time as their falsity may be openly proved before all men."

These contemplations paved the way for the freedom to try out something new and, if it was successful, to expand upon it. There is clear evidence that this led to an industrial revolution in the Middle Ages (J. Gimpel). It provided the economic base for natural sciences and ensured their financial autonomy. The fact that the church consequently came to regard science as a huge threat, repeatedly casting doubt on the principles of liberalism as a prerequisite for independent thought, is another story. At this point, I would like to linger a little longer on the subject of a scientist's approach when searching for truth and his sense of time, as the following quote from R. Dunbar[23] illustrates:

"… their concern is to understand how and why the world is as it is, and if this takes five hundred years of collective effort by a thousand individuals scattered in laboratories all around the world, only a handful of whom ever actually get to meet, then so be it. Success in science comes only from a long slow methodical working through of all the ins and outs of a very complex phenomenon, checking and double-checking everyone else's calculations, because only by patience and careful testing will we avoid mistakes. As the history of science all too often reminds us: nothing is gained by over-hastiness."

2. On ethics: freedom and serfdom

2.1 Definitions and applications of ethics

Derived from the Greek word "ethos" meaning (moral) character or customs, ethics has come to mean the "science of morality", when used in the philosophical sense. Sartre described the term as follows, qualifying ethics as "bourgeois":

"Bourgeois ethics did not derive from Providence; its universal and abstract procedures were inscribed in things." [24]

A. Malraux thought that Buddhism and Christianity were ethical rather than metaphysical religions[25]. M. Weber then explained why protestant Christianity has a greater tendency to produce successful tradesmen than the Catholic Church. By doing so, he showed what enormous influence ethical values can have on the success or the prosperity of a society. D. S. Landes expanded on this theory under the general heading of "culture".

When people were struggling with the choice between "market economy and state-controlled economy" in 1948 and now wrestle with "liberalism or state intervention" today, society has to bear in mind what the consequences might be if they make the wrong decision and how it paves the way for the next generation – with the risk of completely unexpected outcomes emerging from an incalculable complexity.

The 1938 "policy of appeasement" towards Hitler in the middle of the thirty years of warfare from 1914 to 1945 and the war on terrorism since 11 September 2001 are two examples. Can tolerating the persecution of individuals in cohesive societies while condemning torture in one's own country really be reconcilable with the principles of human rights? In B. Beck's introduction to "Le Roman de Renart" I found some examples of Machiavellian tactics used in child rearing:

"From the age of 2 or 3 onwards, the child is subjected to double standards of upbringing based on opposing morals. On the one hand, he is taught concepts inspired by Christianity: don't lie, don't steal, be generous, forgiving, etc., using words that are spoken by the mouth but don't come from the heart. Fearing the child might take these lessons literally and become a fool or a victim, however, he (…) also learns how to win."

What's the situation like in companies? When I asked H. Albert this question, he dismissed the notion of any 'special' business ethics. At the other end of the scale, there are numerous books, including J. Ballot and F. de Bry "L'Entreprise et l'Éthique", that are entirely devoted to this topic. As a general rule, I feel there are good reasons to support the view that there is no need for a 'special ethical practice for business'. In fact, it appears to be superfluous. Perhaps market segmentation, with which 500 tenure-track philosophers in Germany alone occupy their time, is responsible for its emergence. Nevertheless, I would like to briefly mention the natural laws with their fundamental values, as defined by J. Piderit, the former President of the renowned Loyola University in Chicago, in this connection. I will revert to this topic later on.

2.2 Economic requirements

Piderit argues that "efficiency" and "subsidiarity" are the pre-requisites for prosperity and consequently of fundamental importance for the purpose of our discussion:

Efficiency: use of scarce resources

"All goods and services in a society are produced by work. Whether a machine or a person is doing the work, time has been expended if time and personal energy are required to create goods and services. (…) No individual should waste resources. He should marshal his time carefully and make effective use of the goods and services available to him; he should also be concerned that other people do not waste resources, which either he or future generations may wish to use. Natural resources, personal effort, and goods and services should not be wasted without reason. We formalize this principle of social justice by naming it 'the principle of efficiency'."

> **The principle of efficiency:** *Natural resources, personal effort, and commodities and services should not be wasted without good reason.*[26]

Subsidiarity: managing with subsystems

"The fact that people differ in abilities and aspirations … require that the individual, to the extent feasible, should be allowed to pursue the basic goods in the manner she chooses. (…) But the fact also suggests that a person cannot be granted complete freedom,

since in order to help all people attain the essential human goals some coordination of the activities is required. (…) When the group must make a collective decision and cannot defer to the individual, the group should be as small as possible, since this allows the group to weigh the needs, abilities and aspirations of members of this group. (…) Furthermore, if the group functions efficiently, the group decisions reflect the views of most people in the group. (…)"

> **The principle of subsidiarity:** *The coordination and organization of humans and their activities should be designed so that the smallest feasible group regulates its own affairs.*[27]

Freedom: monasteries – cities – merchants

The principles of efficiency and subsidiarity can be used to judge the way of life in monasteries and cities as opposed to life in the villages on the flat land. Their implementation played a substantial role in the rise of new ideas. Piderit fails to recognise the benefits of the concept of competitiveness in the marketplace, however, when he talks about 'cut-throat competition', unlike Hume and Smith. But let us ignore his objection and proceed from the assumption that competition is a natural phenomenon wherever individuals and institutions coexist. People seem to aspire to "greatness". The "greatest" kingdom and the "greatest" cathedral were, as a rule, worthy goals, for instance, even if this often meant rejecting the principles of efficiency and subsidiarity. Feudalism was certainly not one of those forms of political organisation that contributed towards the self-realisation of the individual.

Lots of people accordingly turned their backs on feudalism and took advantage of their hard-won freedom. Economic independence brought wealth. Monasteries and cities, with their merchants, were able to lead their own lives beyond the constraints of feudalism. I would like to expand on this statement with the help of two examples: the Cistercian order and the city of Venice.

T. F. Klein commented as follows on the Cistercian order under the title of "Den Boden umgraben und die Bäume fallen" (Dig the ground and fell the trees):

"By rejecting the feudal system, something that was completely untypical for the time, the Order positioned itself to a certain extent outside the legal norms."

With the help of rich, usually feudal, sponsors, who likewise created more leeway for themselves in this way, the modest beginnings in the solitude of Clairvaux, Burgundy in 1098 evolved to a widespread European movement with 750 monasteries being set up in total, 300 of which were founded in Germany alone. This number doubled with the launch of women's convents. This achievement was largely due to the efforts of Bernard of Clairvaux (1091–1153), who made the Order very attractive for the sons of noble birth and promoted his idea all over Europe. His struggle against Abelard, however, marked the beginning of the demise of intellectual liberty, even in the monasteries. His support for the crusades, in particular, invites considerable criticism.

The following account of medieval cities was written by L. Benevolo:

"The population of the emerging towns, the majority of which had always been made up of merchants and artisans, attempted to escape the feudal system and create appropriate conditions for an economic existence. This essentially included self-government, their own jurisdiction and a progressive fiscal system, with which to finance public spending – predominantly for fortification complexes and arms."

The municipal government bodies, which he identified as forerunners of the present-day constitutional state, consisted of the aldermen, the council and the guilds. There were also religious organisations and, occasionally, an institutional mediator. Early examples include Amalfi[28], still under Roman rule, Venice, Pisa and Genoa. The mercantile city state of Venice was completely unaffected by feudal structures. Another example is Nuremberg, a city that belonged to the citizens and local industry.

Cities were moderately sized and far apart. Asselmey and Schlüter recorded no more than 82 agglomerations in Central Europe in the year 900, over half of which were in Germany. Cities played a key role in the early days of liberalism, which in my opinion provided the impetus for economic growth. The 1980 edition of the Brockhaus encyclopaedia contains the following entry on municipal law ("Stadtrecht"):

"Municipal law is the law that originated in towns and cities (…), which differed from the imperial constitution based on feudal principles. (…) Associations with autonomous legislative powers (guilds etc.) grew up in the towns. 'Town air makes you free' was a common saying in many towns."

Cities competed with one another, thus creating the psychological prerequisites for accepting new ideas. Travelling from one town to another was difficult, however, due to the lack of good roads. In the spring and autumn, rainfall frequently turned the roads to mud so that they became impassable.

Long-distance communications

Most of the news was spread by word of mouth. Reading and writing were reserved for just a privileged few. Noblemen accounted for just 1 per cent of the population, which still did not mean that a basic education was available, however. In 1500, a message took six days to travel from Brussels to Innsbruck, and one month from Augsburg to Madrid. It took two weeks to Venice and half that time to Vienna. In spite of these long delivery times, important news reached all corners of Europe within the space of six weeks[29].

Reputation of merchants

In the Contemporary English Version of Shakespeare's play "The Merchant of Venice", by Jonathan Star, Salarino expresses what the general public thought of merchants, saying:

"My breath, cooling my broth,
Would blow me to a shiver when I thought
What harm a wind, too great, might do at sea.
Each time I saw the sandy hourglass run,
I'd think of shallow flats and sandy banks,

And see my ship, the Andrew, docked in sand
(…)
Thus, in a word, reduce my worth to naught."

And it was possible to live with the guilds, which were not necessarily in favour of progress, just as it is nowadays with science. T. Kuhn claims scientists are required to bow to the relevant prevailing paradigms, or they should switch their career. The same thing applied to medieval artisans and there are a great many people who do not regard it as immoral.

Even if T. Kuhn did not perceive any problems, I think V. Gadenne, who adopts a critical-rational approach and regards the suppression of criticism as highly unfavourable for the awareness process, is right. There is a saying that you often come across in science and business circles: *"Lead or follow. Or get out of the way."* Focusing on problematic aspects or discussing matters is rarely called for under actual working conditions. *"Comply or explain"* is undoubtedly the better alternative.

Liberal anarchy and legal certainty

Due to the strained relations between clerical and secular rule, the monasteries and cities with their tradesmen had hardly any reason to fear prolonged, intrusive interference on the part of the church or central government authorities. The financially autonomous feudal lords only occasionally exerted influence on the monasteries and cities. They played a more active part in their role as sponsors, however. Not even the church with its combination of religious and secular claims to power was able to assert itself in the majority of cases. This provided the foundations for a "liberal anarchy" spanning three centuries, during the course of which trade, industry and science at new universities were able to flourish. This was fertile ground for new ways of thinking, innovation and invention.

What is liberalism? The 1982 edition of the Brockhaus-Wahrig dictionary supplies the following definition:

"Liberalism, which has its roots in the Age of Enlightenment, (…) is a philosophy of the world, the state and market economy that seeks the greatest possible amount of freedom for the individual, which guarantees the greatest possible progress for society and calls for limitations on the authority of the state through division of power and the individual's right to participate in political decision-making (democracy, parliamentarianism)."

How liberal were the Middle Ages between 1000 and 1350?

At first glance, this appears to be a very provocative question since the Middle Ages are often identified with feudalism. But, to quote an example from our own day and age – even though this may come as a surprise to many people – India is now regarded as a liberal country that has opened up to globalisation, despite the fact that only 10 per cent of the population enjoys a standard of living which is comparable with that of the Western world. Perhaps there was a social class that thought and acted liberally in medieval times, too, even if this represented just a minority. This requires further investigation.

Improving the monetary system – the clergy

Since the financing of trade was crucial, maybe we should take a look at the problems connected with money-making and taxes, which were demonised by the church – a viewpoint that probably dated back to Aristotle. The point I wish to make here is that the spread of literacy and the introduction of agencies simplified trade enormously. Inflation played just a minor role in those days, so people had confidence in the currency. R. Gaettens wrote: *"The long medieval era was spared serious monetary crises"*[30], which constituted one aspect of legal certainty. The depreciation of coinage only commenced in 1458 and, together with the plague, famine and the Hundred Years' war, precipitated the decline of the medieval Renaissance[31]. The dramatic change in the attitude adopted by 13th century theologians was of particular importance. S. Jenks notes in this connection that there were now three arguments in favour of trade, which were the prerequisites for economic expansion[32]:

1. *The merchant does not need to engage in trade out of greed (…) in order to feed himself and his family and to give alms to the poor.*

2. *Profit (…) might (…) be accounted for by the work involved in transporting or finishing the goods, by the merchant's storage costs and transport risk.*

3. *After all, the social effects of trading are not simply favourable but downright indispensable: merchants transport goods from areas where they are plentiful to regions where they are scarce or badly needed.*

2.3 Headlines spanning four centuries 1000–1350

Which significant events took place in the Middle Ages, i.e. in the centuries dealt with in this section? A. Peters lists the following occurrences concisely, summing them up in a few words:

1000 The Pope's claim to supreme, universal authority led to battles with emperors and kings.

Freedom due to power vacuum

Crusades delivered Christian Europe from its mediocrity thanks to its encounter with more advanced heathen cultures.

New knowledge through travel

1050 An Inca state based on communism was founded in South America. Socialist ideas were implemented in China.
God was presented as the builder of the universe (see page 145).

Public welfare before private interest *(Contrat Social)*

Printing with moveable letters. Musical notation was born.

Written language for transfer of knowledge in trading

1100   Growth of cities broke through the constraints of Central European village life.

City air provided freedom for critical thinking

The bourgeoisie was made up of merchants and artisans.

Financial independence for economic liberalism

Guilds were set up.

Minimum standards assured by collective action

1150   The orderly translation of Arabic books into Latin paved the way for Europe's academic and scientific advancement.

Science based on rationality

The church launched the Inquisition.

Start of repression: fascism

China introduced standard written characters.

Possibility of imitation

1200   End of the Toltecan Empire in South America. The Mongols marched from the Yellow Sea and advanced into Central Europe to create the biggest empire of all time. Having conquered the Arab Empire, the Mongols retreated to restore their rule in China.

The Turks established their Ottoman Empire in Asia Minor.

Fear and defence: technical progress

1250 The Catholic Church burned its opponents and waged crusades against Christian communities.

Systemisation of oppression

Foundations of experimental science in England.

Freedom of systematical thinking bears fruit

Gothic style replaced Romanesque architecture.

Rationalism of a (still) open society

Invention of spectacles.

Man strove to perfect himself with the help of technology

1300 Italian artists began to revive the free culture of pre-Christian antiquity (Renaissance).

The knowledge of humanity was reactivated

Attempts to reform ecclesiastical jurisdiction coincide (…) with social revolutionary movements.

Contrat Social *(1337–1453, Hundred Years' War)*

1350 Mighty guildhalls announced a rise in bourgeois self-confidence.

Freedom from feudalism

The quest for universal education led to the foundation of universities in numerous cities.

N. Oresmius: "Tractatus de Moneta" (Treatise on Money 1358)

Knowledge is power and freedom

2.4 Thomas Aquinas (1225–1274): a philosopher of the Enlightenment?

According to F. Seibt, the Dominican professor Thomas Aquinas, who was the son of a count, was already teaching the logical coherence of our knowledge:

"The fact that the Thomistic epistemology with the theorem 'cognoscere sequitur esse', 'knowing follows being' or 'epistemology follows ontology', essentially preceded Kant's Category Theory by centuries and basically forged a link to the philosophy of the Enlightenment, (…) may provide insight into the cohesion of European thought."

2.5 Natural law in the Catholic Social Doctrine

According to J. J. Piderit, whom we have already encountered earlier in this essay in connection with the terms efficiency and subsidiarity, we can appraise the development of the Catholic Social Doctrine in the light of seven basic natural law values:

Knowledge
Beauty
Life
Friendship
Playfulness
Practical Reasonableness
Religion

Piderit claimed that the basic values could not be hierarchised although he admitted that, for some people, the basic value of "Religion" has no meaning, so they would manage with just six basic values. I would like to see the basic value of "Life" at the top of the list because what would the other values be without life? The basic value of "practical reasonableness" acts as his joker for explanations whenever he gets stuck. The basic value of "practical reasonableness" could be regarded as a bridge between "natural law" and "rational law".

The other basic values also occasionally invite contradiction, as is the case with most notions put forward by philosophers and ethicists, who appear to be quite unable to find a common denominator – with the result that they frequently confuse scientists and entrepreneurs. According to Büchner[33] it is possible to formulate a plea to philosophers and ethicists in the following words:

"And give us a comfortable religion." This unfortunately leads us from pluralism, which nobody likes, to totalitarianism, which we don't want. So it looks as if we will have to live with contradictions.

Liberty, equality, fraternity – the three ideals of the French Revolution which, as a result of the Philosophy of the Enlightenment and, in particular, J.-J. Rousseau's "Contrat Social", initially put paid to the "Ancien Regime" – are not mentioned at all in Piderit's writings. How do they fit in? And what about the concepts of truth, justice and wealth? Where is there any mention of order?

Piderit approaches the majority of these concepts via the basic value of "practical reasonableness" and ten principles of justice. He divides the latter into four principles for <u>personal</u> justice and six for <u>social</u> justice, to which I have added my own notes:

The principles of personal justice

   Observation of the (seven) core values
   Personal freedom
   Action (reaction)
   Public welfare

The principles of social justice

Subsidiarity
Liberty
Distribution of wealth and income
Efficiency
Responsibility
Impartiality

As Piderit sees it, "fraternity" belongs to the basic value of "friendship", "truth" to the basic value of "knowledge" and "order" to the basic value of "practical reasonableness" or the principle of "efficiency". But where does "liberalism" belong? There is only room in this essay to touch on these matters instead of giving them the special attention they deserve.

Justice: the principles of efficiency

We inevitably come to liberalism when we examine the efficiency of different economic systems. Only a liberal economic regime can lead to an economic miracle, as happened in Germany following the 1948 monetary reform. It doesn't bear thinking about what might have happened if the socialist dream of a state-controlled economy had come true 60 years ago. The politician Friedrich Merz stressed the beneficial effects of lifting the emergency accommodation measures (to cope with the post-war housing crisis and the influx of refugees) in 1964.

Efficiency also means that natural resources, individual effort, commodities and services should not be wasted without good reason.[34]

Piderit's conclusions are qualified by Küng who wants not only human rights but also human responsibilities declared as binding values, or by F. Engels' observations on the moral diversity among different societies – a thought that is now all the more explosive in view of the discussion about the morality of Western civilisation and the morality of Islam[35]:

"What morality is preached to us to-day? There is first Christian-feudal morality, inherited from past centuries; and this again has two main subdivisions, Roman Catholic and Protestant moralities, each of which in turn has no lack of further subdivisions, from Jesuit-Catholic and Orthodox-Protestant to "loose" advanced moralities. Alongside of these we find the modern bourgeois morality, and with it, too, the proletarian morality of the future ..."

2.6 The period around 1250

This was the Great Awakening era which produced some of the finest examples of Gothic architecture and marked the height of the medieval industrial revolution, until several sections of the (tallest) cathedral in Beauvais on the outskirts of Paris, work on which was begun in 1247 and whose nave soars to a height of almost 158 feet, collapsed. The stained-glass windows, dating back to the 13th century, are regarded as historical artistic treasures.

But why did all this fall into decline? This question also needs to be expounded in depth elsewhere. No further progress was made until the Italian Renaissance (1460), and then there was another period of stagnation which lasted until the dawn of the Age of the Enlightenment (1750). Apart from the Hundred Years' War, plague and the climate also played a role, but the main cause was the legal uncertainty and the absence of a constitution that might be implemented by a hegemonic administration. The State was weakened and liberal anarchy had been replaced by secular resignation.

2.7 Two political tragedies: the constitution

The Nobel laureate J. Buchanan aired some of Rousseau's views on the Social Contract in the summer of 2001 in Alpbach, differentiating between two political tragedies:

(1) people normally act in an egoistic manner so, instead of natural anarchy, they need a form of governance that limits personal initiative and makes coexistence possible in the first place, but

(2) this 'governance' needs to levy taxes to cover the costs incurred by its activities if it is to govern the people well. Every government tends to increase this revenue over and above its actual needs, which results in financial losses. People then feel patronised and no longer able to act on their own authority. The principles of subsidiarity and efficiency are undermined and lead to resignation, thus opening the floodgates to totalitarian rule.

According to Buchanan, it is possible to find a compromise and more or less get to grips with the dilemma by means of a 'good', sound constitution and the concerted efforts of several parallel institutions, such as charities, associations and societies, all competing against each other. A constitution regularly needs to be adapted to changing circumstances. Qualified majorities are required. Question: How much of this can be applied to the Middle Ages?

The situation that Ortega described at the turn of the first millennium was without doubt a lawless world, in which hardly anyone appeared to be prepared to take the initiative in matters of any kind, since efforts were not rewarded. There was still a long way to go to the year 1250, and even longer to the present day and age, by which time M. Riedel optimistically claims that, over the course of the centuries, the world would be …

"… *freed from the evils of political arbitrariness and lawlessness, and the idea of the best kind of constitution based on common justice would be realised on the foundations of the modern world*".[36]

3. Résumé and unresolved questions

Evidence of the roots of liberal thought and natural science, which belong together and, in my view, form the basis for freedom and progress, can be found in some monasteries, many cities and, above all, in connection with merchants, building contractors and some philosophers in the Middle Ages. The aim of the essay is to indicate where we might make a start if we want to solve the following questions, in particular:

The influence of legal certainty.
   What laws and charters existed in the feudal system?
   When and where was reliable legislation enacted?[37]

What role did wars and crusades play?

Transfer of Greek knowledge via the Arabs.
   Was there an enlightenment, a pursuit of truth?
   How and why did literacy evolve?

Why did monks start working (work ethic)?
   What was the range of merchandise for which people
      worked?
   How did reliable currency and prosperity evolve?

What role did trade and transportation play?[38]
   How did productivity evolve?
   How safe were travel and transport?

What caused the population explosion between 700 and 1400?

Who introduced new ideas into the world?
  Why were new ideas copied?
  What were the ambitions that seized monasteries and
    cities?

What role did religion and the church play?
  What were the ethics behind it?
  Did people believe in a natural law?
  What role did reason play?

These questions are undoubtedly the responsibility of philosophy and, accordingly, ethics when it reflects on the economy of the High Middle Ages. In his remarkable essay to mark the bicentenary of I. Kant's death on 12 February 2004 entitled "Reason on the brink of the abyss of ignorance – what does it mean to be guided by thought?" D. Henrich defines the role of philosophy as follows:[39]

"Philosophy focuses primarily on the tensions that are merely obscured, but not explored, in the different cultures' ways of viewing the world and their concepts of life. It accordingly attracts all the underlying, puzzled queries that also spawned the primary need for an explanation of the world and of life, with the consequence that the discipline of scientific justification also gradually unfurls within its scope."

There is undoubtedly still a lot to be done in this field of research, at least with regard to the period we are dealing with and from the point of view of an entrepreneur and scientist.

4. Literature

H. Albert: "Kritischer Rationalismus", Tübingen 2000

J. Ballett and F. de Bry: "L'Entreprise et l'Éthique", Paris 2001

B. Beck (ed.): "Le Roman de Renart", Paris 1962

L. Benevolo: "Die Stadt in der europäischen Geschichte", Munich 1999

I. Berlin: "Four Essays on Liberty", Oxford 1969

M. Borgolte: "Europa entdeckt seine Vielfalt 1050 – 1250", Stuttgart 2002

J. Buchanan, H. Kliemt and U. Steinvorth: "Democracy and the Market Economy. The Philosophy of Freedom, Order and Justice", Lecture "Politics as Tragedy", Alpbach 2001

D. Cariou: "La Méditerranée au XIIe Siècle", PUF Paris 1997

K. Deschner: "Kriminalgeschichte des Christentums – Das 11. und 12. Jahrhundert", Reinbek 1999

R. Dunbar: "The Trouble with Science", London 1995

V. Gadenne: "Zur Aktualität von Karl Poppers kritischem Rationalismus", plenary lecture Alpbach 2002

C. Gauvard, A. de Libera and M. Zink: "Dictionnaire du Moyen Age", Paris 2002

D. Gilcher: "Leuchtendes Mittelalter – Rheinische Zisterzienser im Spiegel der Buchkunst", catalogue, Rheinpfalz 25.11.1998

J. Gimpel: "La Révolution Industrielle du Moyen Age", Paris 1975

J. Le Goff: "À la Recherche du Moyen Age", Paris 2003

T. F. Klein: "Den Boden umgraben und die Bäume fäl-
len – Brandenburg und die Geschichte der Zisterzienser" (Dig the ground and fell the trees), FAZ
18.06.1998

W. König (ed.): "Propyläen Technikgeschichte", Frankfurt
1991

T. S. Kuhn: "Die Entstehung des Neuen", 5th edition, Frankfurt 1997

D. S. Landes: "The Wealth and Poverty of Nations", New
York 1998

J. Meran: "Wirtschaftsphilosophie", 2nd edition, FernUniversität Hagen 2000

M. North (ed.): "Deutsche Wirtschaftsgeschichte" (German
Economic History), Munich 2000

J. Ortega y Gasset: "Das Jahr 1000" (The Terrors of the Year
1000), Leipzig 1992

A. Peters: "Synchronoptische Weltgeschichte – Zeitatlas",
Munich 2002

J. J. Piderit: "Ethical Foundations of Economics", Washington 1993

A. Pieper et al.: "Einführung in die philosophische Ethik",
FernUniversität Hagen 2001

M. M. Postan (ed.): "Cambridge Economic History of Europe – The Agrarian Life of the Middle Ages", Cambridge 1966

H. Schnädelbach: "Probleme der Wissenschaftstheorie. Eine
philosophische Einführung", FernUniversität Hagen
1993

B. Schefold (ed.): "Über N. Oresmius' 'Tractatus de Moneta'
Vademecum zu einem Klassiker der mittelalterlichen
Geldlehre", Düsseldorf 1995

F. Seibt: "Die Begründung Europas", 4th edition, Frankfurt 2003

H. Siebert: "Der Kobra-Effekt", 2nd edition, Stuttgart 2002

H. de Soto: "Freiheit für das Kapital – Warum der Kapitalismus nicht weltweit funktioniert", Berlin 2002

… the causes of the wealth and the poverty of nations –
the grand object of all inquiries of Political Economy.

Malthus to Ricardo, letter dated 26 January 1817
quoted in D. L. Landes (1998) and J. M. Keynes (1920)

Part II:
Legal certainty and prosperity

Abstract

The aim of this essay on "Legal certainty and prosperity" is to demonstrate the vital role played by legislation in the development of our civilisation and our prosperity. Taking a brief definition of terms as a basis, I will proceed to explain its importance based on practical examples of attempts to control commercial risk. These will include: (1) The discourse amongst the crew prior to a shipwreck and the Romans' rules for safety at sea. The fact that rules were broken in times of emergency, such as impending famine, illustrates the relativity of the legal principles as proof of their intrinsic unreliability. We will examine the question of emancipation from the point of view of participants in a discussion, highlighting the role of the stringent, logical line of argument, as is customary in the field of science, in particular. (2) Only "old", established norms and customs that have stood the test of time can be trusted. This leads to concerns regarding the risk of innovations, the consequences of which, by definition, are unforeseeable. U. Beck's scepticism towards the scientific understanding of reality and truth comes into play[40]. (3) In this context, we will look at the dynamism of the medieval industrial revolution and emphasise the importance of insurance. Profit as an easily determinable measure of success plays a significant role and is no longer condemned. Prosperity gains greater recognition.

Recent research has shown that it is impossible to be fully aware of all risks. This situation is aggravated by a dispensation of justice that is often completely unpredictable and appears to be at odds with itself. So we need to ask ourselves whether there is any point in engaging in economic activity any more in the current legal and political climate, particularly as far as small and medium-sized companies are concerned, which are unable to spread risk effectively. Is it still possible to get to grips with the risks lying in wait for smaller companies? This discussion is supported by two quotations – one in favour and one against, which are enclosed in the form of annexes: (1) "Science sheds light on agriculture in the 18th century" by Arthur Conte and (2) "The decline of an industrial nation in 1880" by David S. Landes.

1. Introduction

Following on from the essay on the origins of liberalism in the Middle Ages, the second treatise deals with "legal certainty and prosperity". It was Hernando de Soto's "The Mystery of Capital" (2000) that provided the inspiration for this study. The main focus of de Soto's book is how legal certainty can affect the development of a national economy – either to its advantage or its disadvantage. In other words: without economic and legal transparency, nobody believes in the existence of a constitutional state. No one wants to make any investments in times of uncertainty.

If experience shows that those in power adopt an arbitrary approach to the law and/or the people have no confidence in the jurisdiction, then the scarce entrepreneurial talent available will turn its back on the country or retreat into the risk-free private sector.[41] Financial means and human resources in the non-public sector for research and development are not invested because no entrepreneur can be sure whether he will ever reap the rewards of his efforts.[42] State subsidies don't help or are pocketed as a kind of windfall profit.[43] The decline and fall of the national economy are then inevitable.

Proceeding from the question of what risk means and what risk the lack of legal certainty poses for a small-scale entrepreneur, it is necessary to investigate the origins of trade. We look at the risk faced by Roman seafarers in the winter, the risks associated with innovation and the risks that prevailed in medieval times, by way of examples.

The annexes also refer to the relationship between risk and progress based on examples from the agricultural sector and Great Britain's decline as an industrial nation in 1880.

The influence that dependable currency exerts on prosperity is incorporated in the third essay, because business transactions are only justifiable if secure funds are available. Safe money is, in my opinion, an integral part of every legal certainty.

It can be argued that we here in Europe are living in an increasingly chaotic legal vacuum[44]. The hard-won principles of the constitutional state[45] for which people have been fighting since the Middle Ages – beginning with the Magna Carta (1215), for instance – will become invalid. This will be followed by a decline in moral standards that hold a society together. The recent riots in France, England, in Melilla and Ceuta (Spain), and the Arab Spring serve to illustrate this point.

Due to the uncertainty and opacity of the legal situation, the risk faced by business professionals tends towards the never-ending. Every worthwhile business activity outside large-scale corporations such as multinationals, independent non-governmental organisations (NGOs) and the governments of big countries will cease. Mid-tier businesses will crumble.

The ivory towers in which the representatives of our constitutional institutions often live contribute towards this unfortunate situation. How is a national banker or a European judge supposed to know, or even understand, what would have happened in 1,900 German chemical plants if the REACH[46] legislation had been adopted into European law in its original form?

The key word of "entrepreneurship" is missing from the 2010 Lisbon Agenda. When confronted with this question, it occurred to the chairman of a seminar "Mobilising Europe's Growth Potential" in Alpbach[47] that, in view of the "risk" attached, entrepreneurs could make a good profit as well as benefiting from extensive support in the form of self-employment subsidies, sometimes referred to as the "Me, Inc." programme. It is a strange kind of emergency brake when the industrial commissioner, G. Verheugen, withdraws 60 (in words: sixty) draft bills on the grounds that they are simply superfluous or violate the principle of subsidiarity. It sometimes makes one wonder about the qualification of the staff.[48] Risk becomes too complex to be predictable.

"Risk" evidently embodies a kind of "weasel word" that defies any attempt at rational definition. In "The Open Society and its Enemies" (p. 222), Karl Popper argues that, generally speaking, precise definitions can be dispensed with, as they are a form of prejudice:

"The view that the precision of science and of scientific language depends upon the precision of its terms is certainly very plausible, but it is none the less, I believe, a mere prejudice."

Ludwig Wittgenstein also claimed that the meaning of words lay in their usage. And in his book "The Sociology of Risk" Niklas Luhmann needed 32 pages just to define the meaning of the word "Risk".

So, in this essay, I will proceed in a pragmatic manner, using examples to illustrate the *effect* risk has on traders and focusing on legal risks. In doing so, I am following in the footsteps of Hernando de Soto and Toby E. Huff, who attribute the favourable economic development in the industrial nations to the existence of reasonably dependable legal structures.

My treatise on the origins of liberalism in the Middle Ages ended with an outlook: *Evidence of the roots of liberal thought and natural science, which belong together and, in my view, form the basis for freedom and progress, can be found in some monasteries, many cities and, above all, in connection with merchants, building contractors and some philosophers in the Middle Ages.* I will now attempt to elucidate how legal certainty, and the risk reduction that goes hand-in-hand with it, affect the economy. In spite of the reservations mentioned above, the following section elaborates a little on the term "risk".

2. The term "risk"

The first step is to clarify what is understood by "risk". What is meant by the economic risk that merchants were taking in the period around 1250, for instance? What did the structural risk, which led to the collapse of the vaults of the chancel of Beauvais Cathedral in 1284, entail? Or, much later, in 1492, when Columbus set off from Spain with three ships but returned with just one single vessel? Does the following remark on anthropology made by the theologian Gottfried Seebass also fit into the concept of risk?

"Stupidity, narrow-mindedness, mental laziness or irrationality on the part of the active parties are psychological accidents forming part of the conditions which restrict the application of the model to the normal human case and should be taken into account when formulating practical imperatives and (theoretical) norms."[49]

Brockhaus-Wahrig (1983) opted for a fairly easy solution in terms of both the definition and the examples, which point to individual responsibility and accordingly introduce the matter of ethics:

Risk ... danger (of loss) Hazard connected with an undertaking, activity. Possibility of unfavourable consequences arising; business risk, risk of accidents; the financial risk is much too big; that is my personal risk; that remains a risk!; a calculated risk; to fear risk; at one's own risk; ... the risk of miscarriage persists; to take a risk, to assume to risk [Ital. *risico*, *risco*; risicare "to expose oneself to danger, to take a chance"; vulg. Lat. *risicare* "to avoid pitfalls"; Gk. *rhiza* "root, rock/ cliff"]. Romeike sees the term "risk" used variously in economics, law/ jurisprudence, psychology, medicine or engineering sciences.

"Culture" also plays a role: whilst the term is used mainly in a negative sense in German, "risk" in English can be used to describe either negative or positive deviations. The maze of terms and definitions is hardly surprising since modern society is a thicket of risks and chances.

With regard to the problem of "defining a term", Popper discovered that it inevitably led to people going round in circles – a situation that was best resolved by discussing and "comprehending" it. To my mind, this approach echoes the hermeneutical method of (ideal) discourse favoured by Habermas. So, instead of pursuing the question of definitions, I will content myself with the Brockhaus-Wahrig version – with one exception: the definition of the term communication, as employed in Information Science, because disruptions in communications have always increased the risk. The 1960 edition of the Encyclopaedia Britannica explains 'Communication' very simply:

"**Communication.** *In its general application this term denotes the interchange of information by any means. In military language it has two more or less distinct meanings. It denotes the methods by means of which information is conveyed from one person to another by visual signals, telephone, telegraph, radio, television or other mediums. (…) The term also refers to transportation routes for moving troops and supplies, …*"

"Communication" is only used as an introduction to the more general term of "information", to which three pages are dedicated, including references to the US Information Agency and the Information Theory. It is not possible to explore all these details at this point, however.

3. Examples of risks

3.1 Roman seafaring in the winter

When the captive Paulus (10 – 64 AD) was being taken to the court in Rome, the ship was forced to take shelter from the storm. Once in the harbour, talks were held to decide how best to continue their voyage, because the risk of a shipwreck was not left to the responsibility of one individual – the captain – in Roman times. Apart from the captain, the centurion, who accompanied Paulus, the crew and passengers, the council also included the prisoner (!). Would it be wiser to spend the winter in this harbour? Paulus, who had already survived one shipwreck, advocated caution, but the others were more in favour of seeking a better harbour. The ship was subsequently stranded off the coast of Malta[50].

Pliny the Elder recorded that "the spring opens up the ocean to seafarers". In the 4th century A. D. Vegetius divided the year into four seafaring seasons:

(1) sailing was safe and the ocean was open to everyone from 27 May to 14 September;
(2) care should be taken during two uncertain periods: from 10 March to 27 May, and
(3) from 14 September to 11 November, particularly in view of the storms during the equinoxes,
(4) following which the ocean was closed to shipping during the perilous winter months.

However, numerous texts show that it was not always possible to adhere to these recommendations, as it was absolutely imperative to transport grain to Rome or Constantinople in the winter, too, to avert famine and a general uprising among the population.

The risk involved in the case of the voyage undertaken with Paulus, the captive, was subject to discussion. We don't know whether this 'discourse' was conducted in the manner prescribed by Kant[51], however. Niesen differentiates between three forms of discourse in Kant's writings:

- Human right to communicative freedom
- The right to political speech
- The use of free public reason

It is possible that not everyone participating in the discourse was "emancipated" in the Kantian sense of the word, since Niesen stressed that this was an ideal. This emancipation was only within the commoners' reach in times of an absolute power vacuum. Everyone should be able to encounter others on the same epistemic level[52], as well as being adequately informed and capable of responding on equal terms. At least, this was probably not so pronounced in the case of the crew and the passengers as it was with the captain. In this connection, it would be better to refrain from "the pathological phenomenon of communication" via the media.

No doubt the way "risk" was handled in the days of Paulus was just as arbitrary as R. Dunbar describes in his account[53]. In his view, the logical rigour with which scientific arguments are pursued is often beyond the grasp of individuals without the relevant training. Indeed, these precise lines of argument sometimes strike the man-in-the-street as "inhuman".

To the layman, scientists seem more like robotic calculating machines, such as Star Trek's Mr Spock, than real living people. As Aristotle recognised as long ago as the 4th century B. C., people have trouble with rationality and need a helping hand. Dunbar quotes several examples, including a number of studies carried out by Tversky and Kahneman, which I would like to mention here: Wason's Selection Task, cost/benefit analysis, probabilistic questions, statistical problems and the failure to recognise analogies. He believes that although errors of this kind are unlikely to lead to serious problems in everyday life, they can be disastrous in the world of science:

"Science's success hinges on a very rigorous application of the principles of logical deduction and the meticulous testing of hypotheses. (…) Although these processes derive from common sense, the rigour with which they are applied in science is genuinely unnatural."

I feel that Benedict XVI's response to the remonstration that Jesus could not be seen although he was supposed to be present also fits into this discussion. The Pope said there were lots of things that were essential but likewise invisible – such as our reason, or our intelligence, and electricity. What he forgot to mention, however, was that this amounted to an invalid comparison between "apples and oranges". This is an example of a false analogy or unfair dialectic, designed to put people "off the scent".

It seems to me that we are dealing with a problem about "risk" and "progress" and "democracy", where none of us are experts and so we cannot conduct the discourse effectively in the Habermasian sense.[54] Or, as computer specialists like to put it: "Garbage in, garbage out".

But there is also the problem of prosperity or rather what brings about prosperity as a prerequisite for the unimpeded evolution of science. It is the entrepreneurial success which, as we are all aware, entails risk that plays the decisive role in this connection. That is what entrepreneurship[55] is all about. An essential aspect of being an entrepreneur is innovation. So it is necessary to clarify just what is meant by innovation.

3.2 Risks attached to innovation

What is meant by innovation? This term is employed in different ways in the fields of sociology and economics. According to the Brockhaus encyclopaedia, innovation refers to:

"Scientific/technical, cultural or social issues (such as inventions, institutions, ideas, behavioural patterns) and their introduction or dissemination, which alter the social structure of a society in the sense of advancement. Innovation research examines the prerequisites for the creation, diffusion, control (innovation strategies) and effect (social conflicts, improvements in social circumstances) of innovation. In science, the term (…) denotes changes in a system brought about through the deliberate planning and application of evolutionary concepts.

In economics (…) the planning, generation and implementation of new products and product qualities, novel production techniques, new methods of organisation and management as well as the opening of new procurement and sales markets. Although innovation often follows invention, it frequently takes it further by employing a more economical approach.

Until the 18th century, inventions or discoveries were usually the work of practitioners such as artisans or craftsmen[56]; since then they have increasingly become an achievement of scientific research, in which technical imagination and coordinating skill are still of relevance. The research institutes (…) take great pains to organise research."

Schumpeter, Popper, Kuhn, Feyerabend and Lakatos were truly committed to the "Logic of Research" – to echo one of Popper's well-known book titles. An innovation or discovery can only be recognised as such if the state-of-the-art is known. Status reports are of great assistance in this connection. If patents are filed relatively seldom, they can hardly serve to reflect the current situation. One thing is certain, however, and that is the powerful incentive the granting of international patent rights had on innovative activity since 1883, sometimes generating quite substantial financial benefits during the 20-year validity of the patent. This is another pertinent example of how legal certainty is capable of accelerating progress. The question is, however, why intellectual property can become common property within such a short time, whereas the works of artists enjoy exclusive status for much longer and tangible property rights not only last 'forever' but are only subject to inheritance tax?

In his book entitled "Risk Society – Towards a New Modernity" (Risikogesellschaft – Auf dem Weg in eine andere Moderne) U. Beck expounds the risks of innovation at great length, while strongly criticising the reliability of our knowledge. Special attention should be paid to the chapter on "Science beyond Truth and Enlightenment? Reflexivity and Critique of Techno-Scientific Development". Is it at all possible to draw up a status report if the tremendous amount of information has to be taken into account? H. Lübbe asked this (1983) in this connection. Beck went even further:

"The access to reality and truth, which was imputed to science at first is replaced by decisions, rules and conventions which could just as well have turned out differently."

3.3 Risks in medieval times[57]

Many people fled from feudalism and took advantage of their newly-won freedom, which brought economic independence and wealth. Monasteries and cities, with their merchants, were able to lead their own lives beyond the constraints of the feudal system and managed to achieve a reasonable degree of legal certainty. I would like to illustrate this with the help of two examples: the Cistercian monasteries and the city of Venice.

T. F. Klein commented as follows on the Cistercian order under the title of "Den Boden umgraben und die Bäume fallen" (Dig the ground and fell the trees):

"By *rejecting the feudal system, something that was completely untypical for the time, the Order positioned itself to a certain extent outside the legal norms.*"

With the help of rich, usually feudal, sponsors, who likewise created more leeway for themselves in this way – as mentioned in Part I (see page 9) – the modest beginnings in the solitude of Clairvaux, Burgundy in 1098 evolved to a widespread European movement with 750 monasteries being set up in total, 300 of which were founded in Germany alone. This number doubled with the launch of women's convents.

The following account of medieval cities was written by L. Benevolo:

"*The population of the emerging towns, the majority of which had always been made up of merchants and artisans, attempted to escape the feudal system and create appropriate conditions for an economic existence. This essentially included self-government, their own jurisdiction and a progressive fiscal system, with which to finance public spending – predominantly for fortification complexes and arms."*

The municipal government bodies, which he identified as forerunners of the present-day constitutional state, consisted of the aldermen, the council and the guilds. There were also religious organisations and, occasionally, an institutional mediator. Early examples include Amalfi[58], still under Roman rule, Venice, Pisa and Genoa. The mercantile city state of Venice was completely unaffected by feudal structures. Another example is Nuremberg, a city that belonged to the citizens and local industry.

Cities were moderately sized and far apart. Asselmey and Schlüter recorded 82 agglomerations in Central Europe in the year 900, over half of which were in Germany. Cities played a key role in the early days of liberalism, however, which in my opinion provided the impetus for economic growth. The 1980 edition of the Brockhaus encyclopaedia contains the following entry on municipal law ("Stadtrecht"):

"Municipal law is the law that originated in towns and cities (…), which differed from the imperial constitution based on feudal principles. (…) Associations with autonomous legislative powers (guilds etc.) grew up in the towns. 'Town air makes you free' was a common saying in many towns."

Cities competed with one another, thus creating the psychological prerequisites for accepting new ideas. In the

Contemporary English Version of Shakespeare's play "The Merchant of Venice", by Jonathan Star, Salarino expresses what the general public thought of merchants, saying:

> *My breath, cooling my broth,*
> *Would blow me to a shiver when I thought*
> *What harm a wind, too great, might do at sea.*
> *Each time I saw the sandy hour-glass run,*
> *I'd think of shallow flats and sandy banks,*
> *And see my ship, the Andrew, docked in sand*
> *(…)*
> *Thus, in a word, reduce my worth to naught.*

But insurance was already mentioned in the 8th century during the reign of King Charlemagne, and again in 1063 in the first maritime law of the Middle Ages "Ordinamenta et consuetudo maris" (Ordinances and Custom of the Sea), drawn up in Trani in 1255 in the Venetian maritime law and one year later, in 1256, in the Statute of Marseille. Compulsory insurance lessened the risk.[59]

The monetary system had developed sufficiently since the end of the 11th century so trade was now much easier.[60] In view of the numerous innovations – including non-metallic currency, paper money, in other words – M. Bloch even spoke of a "monetary revolution".[61] Financing trade was of considerable importance, so perhaps we should devote some time to the problem of money-making, which was demonised by the church – presumably based on Aristotle's teachings – as well as the aspects of interest, risk and profit. One thing is clear, though: the spread of literacy and the introduction of agencies simplified trade enormously. As suggested above, inflation only played a minor role in those days, so people were able to place their trust in the currency and could afford to be confident about their economic future. In the words of R. Gaettens: *"The long medieval era was spared serious monetary crises."*[62] This constituted one aspect of legal certainty and accordingly a decrease in risk. The depreciation of coinage only commenced in 1458 and, together with the plague, famine and the Hundred Years' War, precipitated the decline of the medieval Renaissance[63]. The dramatic change in the attitude adopted by 13th century theologians was of particular importance. S. Jenks notes in this connection that there were now three arguments in favour of trade, which were the prerequisites for economic expansion as they paved the way for profit-making and offset the risk that goes hand-in-hand with trading of any kind[64]:

1. *The merchant does not need to engage in trade out of greed (…) in order to feed himself and his family and to give alms to the poor, for example.*

2. *Profit (…) might (…) be accounted for by the work involved in transporting or finishing the goods, by the merchant's storage costs and transport risk.*

3. *After all, the social effects of trading are not simply favourable but downright indispensable: merchants transport goods from areas where they are plentiful to regions where they are scarce or badly needed.*

Traders felt times were particularly difficult and the prospects of making a profit were left to chance. Working in the wholesale or retail trade was something of an adventure in those days. Anxiety, or rather fear, were the daily lot of merchants like Datini (1335–1410). *Risicum, periculum, fortuna*: these terms (risk, danger, fortune) repeatedly cropped up in trade contracts. It was essential to look for *securitas*. Common sense was called for in order to conduct one's business in a practical, careful and meaningful manner (*per ragione*). The obstacles that merchants were most afraid of were:

- Selling at a loss
- Shipwreck
- Wars
- Taxes
- Lack of trade privileges
- Mistrust on the part of the population

Wholesale merchants displayed international far-sightedness on the one hand, but at the same time they were also dependent on help from local intermediaries who often held the monopoly for selling the imported products. They were unavoidable middlemen when it came to bulk buying. A contemporary of that time came to the following conclusion: "It is profitable when there are free ports!". What meets the eye is the extraordinary increase in regulations, even if they were not always adhered to.[65]

Subsistence farmers cannot afford to take any risks for fear of jeopardising their very existence. Changes are only feasible if there is enough "venture capital". Or, to put it in a nutshell: "If you want to speculate, you need money to spare!" D. S. Landes contemplates what the ideals of a society that ensures universal prosperity and progress might be. Avoiding ethical evaluation, he sets great store by this society being able to provide goods and services. According to Landes, there are five imperatives for accomplishing that aim:

- Using resources efficiently and making improvements
- Passing knowledge on to the next generation
- Only assigning work (tasks) according to performance
- Giving entrepreneurship every conceivable chance
- Using freedom, the fruit of one's work, oneself

Entrepreneurship is inextricably linked to risk. If the 2010 Lisbon Agenda fails to make any mention of this aspect, the European Union cannot be really serious about economic evolution, in my opinion. Nor can it be right to lower corporate tax to 25 per cent of profits in view of international competition, which means that the State only has a 25 per cent share in the risk. A rate of 50 per cent would increase leverage considerably. State intervention becomes absurd if the government pays risk subsidies – for R & D, for example – only to subject them to profits taxes again, or rescues ailing companies like Holzmann, Opel or Karstadt for the time being in order to win the next election. The premium for scrapping older cars that are still roadworthy is the height of incompetence on the part of the politicians.

4. Awareness of risks

The degree of risk justifies the amount of profit. Students of economics are also taught that a risk has to be proportionate to the size of the company, however. The organisation should <u>never</u> be endangered by rushing headlong into any risks. It is this that distinguishes the entrepreneur from the adventurer. What it boils down to is that smaller companies should only take smaller risks in proportion to their resources. But how does one go about estimating the degree of risk involved? What level of information is at the decision-maker's disposal? What can we learn from the past?

The decision-maker has to take five different masses of information into account in order to make an educated guess – whether he is already in possession of all the information he needs or requires further details, in other words. These are variables that more or less overlap each other and, as a general rule, only lead to an incomplete information status (Fig. 1):

1 Availability of information
2 Objective need for information
3 Subjective need for information
4 **Demand** for information
5 **Decision-maker's information status**

In general, however, the information available fails to cover the objective need for information, meaning the details required to make an optimum decision are incomplete. This applies in particular when an urgent decision is called for. The Internet, incidentally, is not of great assistance for optimised decisions in view of its unreliability. Another obstacle is that the decision-maker is not necessarily aware of what he ought to know, as he is only in possession of subjective information. He might possibly think he should know a lot of things that appear to be irrelevant for an optimised decision. In most cases, instead of asking all the necessary questions, he will content himself with a limited erudition within his "subjective" need for information. So his resultant information status may differ considerably from the objective need for information required.[66]

This consequently leads to decisions based on uncertain information (Spies 1993) that might possibly harbour high unknown risks. It is for this reason that some authors choose to write about "Companies (teetering) on the brink of chaos" (Stacey 1997) or "Competing on the Edge – Strategy as Structured Chaos" (Brown and Eisenhardt 1998).

5. Legal certainty – property – contractual freedom

Legal certainty is a vital catalyst for spurring prosperity.[67] It probably even embodies the most important principles of order. M. Schmoeckel provides a fascinating overview.[68] In the words of W. Eucken: "Confusion sets in where thinking in terms of systems of order stops." This is a situation that a businessman cannot cope with, because the word "credit" comes from the Latin credere (to believe or trust). Ever since A. Peyrefitte and N. Luhmann, everyone knows that trust reduces transaction costs enormously.

Property is the second vital prerequisite for the prosperity of a country. According to J. Locke, man has the right of self-ownership (individual liberty) and equal entitlement to use the Earth – which is only limited by God's will. Based on this proviso, everybody could acquire free or common goods through their labour. Even if J. Locke took this for granted, I. Kant put him in his place: "To work on something that is not my property (…) does not lead to ownership in it (its substance), but only to the possession of its accidents."*

Anthony de Jasay suggests that only our collective ownership of everything is legitimate, which is also reflected to a certain extent in the social restrictions on individual property laid down in German Basic Law. Surely we cannot simply accept this claim at face value. It leaves the principle of allocating

---

* See Immanuel Kant, Die Metaphysik der Sitten, Akademieausgabe VI, p. 268f., translation by Hardy Bouillon in his paper "Let loose of Lockeworking". http://www.swissmc.ch/documents/Hardy_Bouillon-Let_loose_of_Lockeworking_paper_9_2010.pdf

responsibility open, and this can probably only be justified by the concept of ownership coupled with the appropriation of ownership.[*]

Once order has been established in the form of legal certainty and the right to the product of one's own labour is ensured by ownership, the road to prosperity is open. Prosperity is the prerequisite for economic independence and, in the broader sense, for emancipation and responsible action. It is only when legal certainty is teamed with prosperity that innovations can emerge on a larger scale. Or, to put it another way: a subsistence farmer is not in a position to risk introducing any innovations. If the innovation in question fails, his livelihood is in jeopardy. D. Benor was not the only person who had a few interesting things to say on this matter on behalf of the World Bank; only recently, J. Sachs also drew attention to this problem.

Since one of the biggest risks facing entrepreneurs is their legal vulnerability with regard to the supposed freedom of contract, even their staff can pose a danger and cost the company's survival. This even applies where advisers are hired, because advisers can be unreliable, incapable or may actually try to defraud their clients. Here are two examples relating to the labour and social law[69]:

Example 1: Safeguarding company secrets is far from simple. Clauses frequently fail to come up to the entrepreneur's expectations. As so often in German company law, there is hardly ever a straightforward solution, and standard confi-

---

[*]   *See Anthony de Jasay, Choice, Contract, Consent: A Restatement of Liberalism (Hobart Paperback 30), London: Institute of Economic Affairs 1991, p. 72.*

dentiality obligations violate the transparency requirements that were introduced as recently as 2003 and apply <u>retro-actively</u>. Members of staff leaving the company might still use the company's client base for their own personal use even though this is prohibited; what the employee mustn't do is sell the lists of customers. Unless post-employment competition restrictions and attendant waiting allowances are agreed, the know-how is left without any form of protection, and the waiting period must not exceed two years[70].

Example 2: According to a decision reached by the District Court of Appeal in Frankfurt, all agreements requiring a director to give back any personal stake in the company that is tied to his executive position should be declared void. It was not until several years later that the Federal Supreme Court (Bundesgerichtshof) succeeded in quashing this decision.

That raises the question whether the risk attached to setting up one's own business might not be too high. Is business only something for fools and rascals, as seen through the eyes of Mark Twain? The Age of the Enlightenment – so full of hope and promise, as described by A. Conte – is a thing of the past (Annex 1); D. L. Landes gives a more realistic picture using Great Britain as an example: the relentless decline of an industrial nation 130 years ago (Annex 2).

Does this also apply to the industrial nation of Germany if it fails to create more jobs in the service sector?

6. Conclusions

In his book "After Virtue: A Study in Moral Theory", A. MacIntyre proves that possible concepts of morality, whether they are supposedly rooted in passions (Hume), reason (Kant) or decision (Kierkegaard), are dubious and their justification comes unstuck.[71] From this I deduce that the fundamental principles of morality were established – in the same way as legislation – by man. It used to be the responsibility of religion, with its stories and parables, to teach people how to live together reasonably harmoniously with the help of sensibly defined morals; nowadays, it falls to politics to assume that role. Human rights are a good example. If morality is man-made, just like the laws, then it is the entrepreneur's duty to run his organisation as efficiently as possible within this framework in order to ensure the company's long-term survival. This takes place in the context of "normal" interpersonal behaviour, which we can call morality, and in the context of the laws. Within this framework there are bound to be risks, some of which can be covered by insurance. Accordingly, revenue must also serve to cover incalculable risks in the long term. If politics – and the legal system – continue to raise the level of uncertainty, and consequently the risk, with imprudent legislation, then the profits will constantly need to be pushed even higher or the company will drop out of the market – voluntarily or due to bankruptcy. Or, as an economist recently suggested: It is, of course, up to the (national) community to decide whether to extend leisure time – by which he meant, in addition to a lengthy period of education and early retirement, a 35-hour-week with six weeks holiday, two weeks convalescence at a health resort and several weeks sick leave. Taken to an extreme, leisure time is only interrupted by the "work" episode by way of a social activity. The community then has to face both the foreseeable and the unforeseeable consequences. This throws open the flood gates for totalitarian, state-controlled economies to flourish when democracy fails. MacIntyre elaborates on the concept of systematic unpredictability in human affairs by employing the term "Fortuna" in the same way as Machiavelli. He names four sources of uncertainty:

(1) *Radical innovation, like the invention of the wheel, is not predictable.*
(2) *I myself as an individual do not know in advance which option I will take, so I am unable to foresee my own future.*
(3) *Game-theoretic considerations: players are not rational.*
(4) *Pure contingency, just as Cleopatra's beauty may have been the cause of the founding of the Roman Empire*[72].

In the eyes of both MacIntyre and Beck, this situation leads to the hostility a society displays towards innovations, which dates back to ancient times. According to H.-J. Quadbeck-Seeger, former Research Director at BASF:

"*Look: Socrates and Plato both went in search of the true, good and beautiful. Not that which is new. New ideas and inventions have long been neglected in our cultural environment. In fact, people are afraid of innovation. Fear is no doubt part of our evolutionary heritage. In former times, fear was an advantage in the fight for survival.*"

A headline in the Frankfurt Allgemeine newspaper (FAZ) reads: "The others do the experiments; we take care of the ethics."[73] This is the reason why the laws laid down by politicians appear to be biased against enterprise and consequently against affluence. Growth, which improves circumstances for everyone, is often dispensed with for ideological reasons.

The exhibition "Chance: Risk – for a venture culture – Life – a venture", which was staged on the occasion of the 125th anniversary of the Münchener Rück insurance company in 2005, provided an excellent overview on this topic. The organisers wrote: *"The willingness to take a chance is the motor that drives all economic and social development. The aim of this brochure is to promote more venture culture and risk propensity and open people's eyes to the chances risk has to offer."* But then it is up to the State to create a more stable setting. The opposite is true. The danger of negative financial trends, such as inflation, devaluation, etc., was not considered as a risk at all in the aforementioned essay.

This leads me to the conclusion that – without adequate insurance – the risk of setting up a small/mid-tier business no longer seems feasible. Every risk analysis demonstrates that we don't know enough to make dependable decisions. Assuming we decide to take the risk, either we face the threat of fiscal expropriation as soon as the business prospers, or our heirs do at some later stage. An unpredictable jurisdiction plays a mere supporting role (see Annex "Assessors as judges?"), acting as a poor substitute for clear, comprehensible laws. Brigitte Kronauer recently spoke of "imperialist" political decisions[74]. This bears a striking similarity to Plato's vision of the ideal State.

7. Literature

U. Beck: "Risikogesellschaft – Auf dem Weg in eine andere Moderne", Frankfurt 2003

L. Benevolo: "Die Stadt in der europäischen Geschichte", Munich 1999

T. Bingham: "The Rule of Law", London 2010

M. Borgolte: "Europa entdeckt seine Vielfalt 1050–1250", Stuttgart 2002

J. M. Broekman: "Recht und Anthropologie", Freiburg 1979

S. L. Brown and K. M. Eisenhardt: "Competing on the Edge – Strategy as Structured Chaos", Boston 1998

H. F. Cohen and T. E. Huff: "Why the West", Seminar Alpbach 2005

P. Contamine et al.: "L'Économie Médiévale", 3rd edition, Paris 2003

D. Dörner: "Die Logik des Misslingens – Strategisches Denken in komplexen Situationen", Reinbek 1999

P. Garnsey: "Thinking about Property – From Antiquity to the Age of Revolution", Cambridge 2007

J. Gimpel: "La Révolution Industrielle du Moyen Age", Paris 1975

G. A. Horn et al.: "Mobilising Europe's Growth Potential", Seminar Alpbach 2005

D. S. Landes: "The Wealth and Poverty of Nations", New York 1998

N. Luhmann: "Soziologie des Risikos", Berlin 2003

A. MacIntyre: "After Virtue: A study in Moral Theory", Frankfurt 1995

Münchner Rück: "Chance: Risiko – Für eine Wagniskultur", Munich 2005

G. Mythen: "Ulrich Beck – A Critical Introduction to the Risk Society", London 2004

M. North (ed.): "Deutsche Wirtschaftsgeschichte" (German Economic History), Munich 2000

J. Pfeffer and R. I. Sutton: "The Knowing-Doing Gap – How Smart Companies Turn Knowledge into Action", Boston 1999

J. J. Piderit: "Ethical Foundations of Economics", Washington 1993

K. Popper: "Die offene Gesellschaft und ihre Feinde II", 7th edition, Tübingen 1992

J. Purdy: "The Meaning of Property – Freedom, Community, and the Legal Imagination", New Haven 2010

F. Romeike: "Lexikon Risiko-Management – 1.000 Begriffe", Cologne 2004

F. Romeike and B. Finke (ed.): "Erfolgsfaktor Risiko-Management – Chance für Industrie und Handel – Methoden, Beispiele, Checklisten", including CD-ROM, Wiesbaden 2003

M. Schmoeckel: "Auf der Suche nach der verlorenen Ordnung – 2.000 Jahre Recht in Europa – Ein Überblick", Cologne 2005

F. Seibt: "Die Begründung Europas", 4th edition, Frankfurt 2003

H. de Soto: "Freiheit für das Kapital – Warum der Kapitalismus nicht weltweit funktioniert", preface by L. Spät, Berlin 2002 ["The Mystery of Capital", New York 2000]

G. Spendel: "Für Vernunft und Recht", Tübingen 2004

M. Spies: "Unsicheres Wissen – Wahrscheinlichkeit, Fuzzy-Logic, neuronale Netze und menschliches Denken", Heidelberg 1993

R. D. Stacey: "Unternehmen am Rande des Chaos – Komplexität und Kreativität in Organisationen", Stuttgart 1997 ["Complexity and creativity in organizations", San Francisco 1996]

J. A. Tainter: "The Collapse of Complex Societies", Cambridge 1988

8. Annexes

8.1 Science sheds light on 18th century agriculture
by A. Conte[75]

… It is not until the 18th century that something is being done to escape the rut of antiquated customs. It is mainly middle-class landowners – sometimes even noblemen – who are leading the movement that is striving to completely revolutionise methods and tools. They are the real pioneers of a new kind of ranch, without being cowboys.

They are convinced that science can shed light on agriculture[76]. They are part of the wave of popular enthusiasm for science. Most of them are members of independent professions. They pursue natural history as others practise philosophy. Sometimes they do both at the same time. This motivates them even more because, as landowners, they are interested in making a profit in a leisurely manner. So they adopt utilitarian ideas: they study in order to conduct trade. They read Noël Pluche, the Count of Buffon, Réaumur, Jean-François Rozier and Duhamel du Manceau. Arthur Young (…) is making a thorough study of the estate belonging to the Count of Liancourt, a kind of model.

These naturalists and agronomists, practitioners and scientists are curious about real life. They are highly interested in the plant cultures on their land. They are prepared to look into the most sophisticated innovations and with all new plants that can be adapted. Not that they are completely selfless: they are aware of the financial aspects. (…) Above all, they are concerned about their income. And, when an opportunity presents itself, they chase the ordinary people off their land.

But they are the only ones who are prepared to carry out experiments that might lead to new work processes. They are seeking to lighten the workload to make toil hard hard for man and beast. They use scientific methods to improve the labour techniques. It is the laboratory that helps the farmers.

8.2 The decline of an industrial nation in 1880
by D. S. Landes[77]

… concerns about Britain's loss of industrial leadership were rejected by many – including many economists – because they could be and were used to challenge the sacred.

An economy built on exports was losing its export markets. In response to labor unions and political pressure, the British government subsidized and socialized the old standbys – iron and steel, cotton textiles, coal. But no growth there. Just unemployed labor, encrusted practices and torturous decline. (p. 453)

… sometimes (…) entrepreneurs retire to a life of interest, dividends, rents and ease. That is also evidence of rationality more than enterprise. One can understand the choice: enterprise is strenuous and risky – who needs it? (p. 456)

… Succession of control is a difficult and invidious process, pitting insiders against outsiders, some insiders against others, blood against talent, blood against blood, talent against talent. (…) at stake, decisions regarding choice of product and methods of production. Here the British were late in exploiting newer fields and ways, stressing instead learning by doing, in the shop and at the bench. Such job apprenticeship has its virtues and successes, but nothing is better calculated to preserve the old in aspic and miss the possibilities of innovation. (p. 457)

… But what about the new branches of manufacture, the industries of the second industrial revolution? (… the defenders of British enterprise have done little with these success stories because they were in fact few and small.) The second industrial revolution misfired. (…) The most egregious failure was the abortion of the protean industry of organic chemicals. (…) Here Britain was actually the pioneer and leader (…) but lost out for want of knowledge, imagination and enterprise to Germany, Switzerland, even France. Management made no commitment to systematic research …

… the absence of any intimate connection or intercourse between our scientific men and our manufacturers. Here one recognizes the extent of British abdication. (p. 457)

8.3 Scepticism towards modernity by U. Beck[78]

[U. Beck: "Risk Society" – Translation © Sage Publications, 1992, page 156. jk]

As a consequence, a momentous *demonopolisation of scientific knowledge claims* comes about: science becomes more and more necessary, but at the same time, *less and less sufficient* for the socially binding definition of truth.

This loss of function is no accident. Nor is it imposed on scientists from the outside. It arises instead as a consequence of the *triumph* and differentiation of scientific validity claims, it is a *product of the reflexivity* of techno-scientific development under the conditions of the risk society.

On the one hand, as it encounters itself in both its internal and its external relations, science begins to extend the methodological power of its scepticism to its own foundations and practical results. Accordingly, the claim to knowledge and enlightenment is systematically scaled back in the face of the *successfully* advanced fallibilism. The access to reality and truth which was imputed to science at first is replaced by decisions, rules and conventions which could just as well have turned out differently.

On the other hand, as science becomes more differentiated, the flood of conditional, uncertain and detached detailed results increases and becomes impossible to survey. This *hypercomplexity* of hypothetical knowledge can no longer be mastered by mechanical testing rules. Even substitute criteria such as reputation, type and place of publication, institutional basis also fail.

Accordingly, as scientization proceeds, the systematically produced uncertainty spreads to external relations, and conversely turns the target groups and appliers of scientific results in politics, business and the public into active *coproducers* in the social process of knowledge definition. The 'objects' of scientization also become *subjects* of it, in the sense that they can and must actively manipulate the heterogeneous supply of scientific interpretation. And this not only means choices between contradictory highly specialized validity claims; the latter can also be played off against one another and must in any case be recombined into an image suitable for action.

For the target groups and appliers of science, reflexive scientization thus opens up *new possibilities of influence and development* in the processes of production and application of scientific results. This is a development of great ambivalence. It contains the opportunity to emancipate social practice *from* science *through* science; on the other hand it *immunizes* socially prevailing ideologies and interested standpoints against enlightened scientific claims, and throws the door open to a *feudalization* of scientific knowledge practice through economic and political interests and 'new dogmas'.

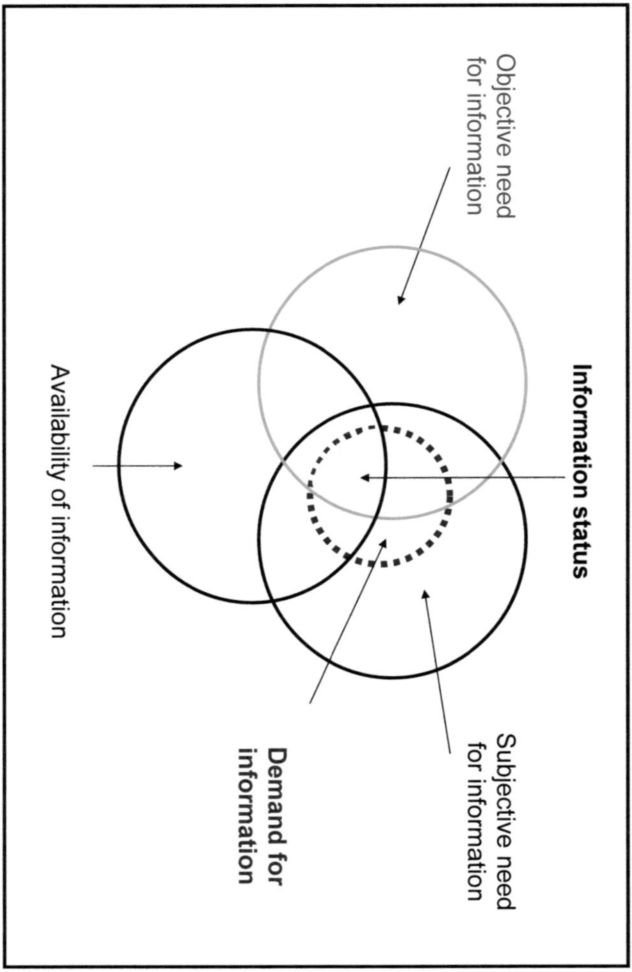

Fig. 3: Decision-maker's information status (Picot and Reichwald, 1991)

The misery of being an expert witness
Assessors as judges? by E. Caspary[79]

The parents are locked in a bitter custody battle for their only daughter. […] The judge decides to call in an expert on psychology to provide a statement to help clarify what would be better for the daughter. […] To the mother's horror, the assessor's testimony favours the father. […]

In the oral proceedings, the expert witness declares that the case was very difficult and he would really have preferred to delegate the task to someone else; he could just as well have decided in the mother's favour, in which case he would have given this or that reason, but he had to make up his mind. After all, on one occasion he had his testimony returned to him because he had failed to make a recommendation. The mother's solicitor is appalled. The judge isn't. He explains that he would also have returned the testimony if the expert had omitted to make any recommendation, because then he (the assessor) would not have fulfilled his obligation. As the solicitor's sense of shock worsens, he points out to the judge that the assessor is only acting as an assistant to the court. He is only supposed to provide unascertainable psychological facts to help the judge – in the absence of pertinent knowledge himself – to find a solution in the child's best interests. It is, however, always up to the judge to decide – not the assessor. […]

Unfortunately, experts are nonetheless … repeatedly forced into the role of the judge – presumably an indication of the excessive demands frequently observed in cases such as these.

Part III:
Opening up to the world around 1000

Catalonia between Christianity and Islam

Abstract

The agricultural region of Catalonia at the base of the Pyrenees opened up to the world around 1000. The economy between Christianity and Islam showed initial signs of globalisation. In the north-east of the Iberian Peninsula, social philosophy has discovered an example of how different cultures can co-exist peacefully and nurture one another if the legal framework is not upset by irrational agitation.

Such aspects as "the blossoming of finance", "acceleration of trade", "the blossoming of production" and "the signs of progress" show how, within the space of just 100 years, external influences that were employed by the government succeeded in turning an extremely poor subsistence economy into one of the most flourishing European civilisations in the Middle Ages. It was during this period that the foundations were laid for Catalonia's current economic boom.[80]

1. Introduction

On the subject of globalisation I would like to deal with one aspect of the medieval economy under the heading of "Opening up to the world around 1000 – Catalonia between Christianity and Islam". This essay pertains to the topic of "The marketplace and the global market – world community", which accordingly acquires a historic perspective. This treatise complements my essays on "Liberalism around the year 1250" and "Legal certainty and prosperity".

This essay was initially motivated by Nicole Oresme's treatise "De Origine et Natura, Jure & Mutationibus Monetarum" on the origin, nature, law and alterations of money (1355), which dealt with the outcomes of the State sliding towards bankruptcy, which amounts to legally sanctioned fraud but is played down as inflation or a monetary downturn. Then I discovered the formidable thèse d'État (doctoral thesis) by P. Bonnassie, University of Toulouse, on the subject of "La Catalogne au tournant de l'an mil" and found the section on the economic growth and the changes in the standard of living in the north-east part of the Iberian Peninsula, with which I am personally well acquainted, of particular interest.

Social philosophy has discovered examples in Catalonia of how different cultures can coexist peacefully and inspire one another provided the basic legal concepts are not destroyed by any irrational agitation. Freimut Duwe remarked on the completely uncalled-for conflict in Yugoslavia, controversies that were avoided in Catalonia.[81]

As Bonnassie's chapter headings:

- Opening up to the world
- The blossoming of finance
- The acceleration of trade
- The blossoming of production
- The signs of progress

already suggest, this is all about how an extremely poor subsistence economy was transformed into one of the most flourishing European civilisations in our collective memory within the space of just 100 years, thanks to external influences which were exploited by the government.

It was around 1000 that the foundations were laid for Catalonia's economic advancement during the Middle Ages and the present day. It would be worth investigating to what extent the economic upswing of this "developing country" can serve as an example for other nations. There can be no doubt that the market's ability to function properly played a decisive role. For this reason, I would like to elaborate a little on the subject of 'market economy'.

2. Justification for the social market economy

The occasionally bemoaned lack of justification for the market economy – in my opinion very misleadingly referred to as 'capitalism' – can be overcome with the help of primatology. According to D. L. Landes, culture involves a tremendous amount of body work, which doesn't come free. There are five imperatives, which I have already mentioned before but am listing again below[82]:

- Using resources efficiently and making improvements
- Passing knowledge on to the next generation
- Only assigning work (tasks) according to performance
- Giving entrepreneurship every conceivable chance
- Using freedom, the fruit of one's work, oneself

S. Freud also thought that every generation of babies was like a barbarian invasion; they were completely lacking in culture, comprehension and discipline. It seems that this anthropologically justifiable cultural work is being sacrificed at the expense of the so-called eligibility of the democratic parties. This leads to a democracy by opinion poll[83]. Yugoslavia can once again be cited as an example. Despite all the help from America and the USSR, the Yugoslav system of workers' self-management has led to chaos. The country's decline was therefore inevitable. In this connection, I would refer to the latest disputes about globalisation.[84]

P. Cahuc et al. devoted considerable thought to the topic of market economy and, in particular, the core issue of competition, and their contemplations are worth considering because they show how disastrous it can be if a populist partitocracy deprives the people of their democratic rights[85,86]. The consequences for the employment market fall far behind the principles of the Catholic Social Doctrine and hinder employees' chances of self-realisation.

> *Every state* intervention *calls for financial means that have to be raised by the people, who may find this redistribution of funds unfair. Boosting the population's efficiency and improving the subsidiary structures – self-help, in other words – are a better solution.*[87]

I proceed from the assumption that every group of people must try to achieve the greatest possible **prosperity for the entire group** while retaining the maximum **level of personal freedom** possible. We should bear in mind, however, that prosperity should be measured in economic units, i.e. in monetary value, as we don't know any better benchmarks, unfortunately.

Money is easy to count.[88] Provided the monetary value remains stable – no fraudulent government inflation, in other words – money lends itself to measuring prosperity. Then prosperity can also be regarded as a godsend and/or as social recognition. Proprietors who lack business acumen or have badly run organisations are eliminated by bankruptcy, making way for an autopoietic process that leads to an ongoing increase in prosperity, as far as taxation and legislation allow. A prosperous society can afford to provide its weaker members with the financial support they need to live a decent life.

> *It would seem that cultural, immeasurable prosperity is subsidiarily based on material wealth.*[89]

Only an increase in prosperity can put a group of people in a position to defend themselves against the interests of other groups – if legislation fails or in the event of a war. Otherwise the interests of the group to which they belong would be damaged or destroyed by the interests of other groups. The majority will prevail simply because it possesses more physical power. W. Hegel goes a lot further with his bellicist remark, advocating war in his "Philosophy of Right"[90]:

"War is that condition in which the vanity of temporal things and temporal goods – which tends at other times to be merely a pious phrase – takes on a serious significance, and it is accordingly the moment in which the ideality of the particular attains its right and becomes actuality."[*]

In his "Phenomenology of Spirit" (sometimes called "Phenomenology of Mind") he wrote[91]:

"War is the spirit and form in which the essential moment of ethical substance, the absolute [sic] freedom of ethical self-consciousness from all and every kind of existence, is manifestly confirmed and realized."[**]

---

[*]   *Source: Elements of the philosophy of right, Georg Wilhelm Friedrich Hegel, Allen W. Wood, p. 361*

[**] *Source: The Phenomenology of Mind, Bilingual, with Dictionary http://www.waste.org/-roadrunner/Hegel C: Free Concrete Mind: (BB) Spirit 3. Dissolution of the Ethical Being*

It is important to recognise the tremendous impact exerted by inflation. Inflation amounts to nothing less than a war waged by the State against the citizens. It is a well-known fact that inflation led to the fall of the Roman Empire. Philipp II of Spain, heir to Charles V, declared state bankruptcy on several occasions. In 1789 France's economic turmoil led to the Revolution, coupled with inflation. Goethe gave a drastic account of the hardship and the introduction of paper money in Faust II. The hyperinflation of 1923 contributed to Hitler's rise to power, and in 1948 there was a surplus of 250 billion Marks to be remedied by the currency reform. The financial crisis led to the collapse of the Marxist Empire: money couldn't buy anything any more. Whenever people lost their faith in the economy, this caused the state government to break down.[92]

Excursus: Inflation in post-war Germany

P. Welter describes the phenomenon of fraud via inflation, the gradual slide towards national bankruptcy, as follows[93]:

"A financial policy that allows high inflation rates is penalised much more swiftly and dramatically nowadays than it used to be by currency devaluation and the flight of capital. (…) In the long or medium term, it is of course not the changes in the real economy that determine inflation but the magnitude of the money supply alone – which in turn points to the central bankers."

What was it like in post-war Germany? Following the decision to reject a state-controlled economy in favour of a market economy, the first three years following 1952 saw no inflation in the trizone. At the end of the next 20 years, however, the currency was only worth half. It took another thirty years to reduce it to a quarter of its 1952 value.[94] In 30 years' time – if everything else remains the same – it will have dropped to a mere eighth of its value. Our present financial assets will have shrunk to half of what they are today unless this can be offset by taxable interest.

1952	100	
1955	100	Three years of stable monetary value
1960	110	
1965	126	
1975	190	Monetary value reduced to half
1985	280	
1995	357	
2005	411	Monetary value reduced to a quarter
2035	800	*Monetary value reduced to an* **eighth**

Inflation in post-war Germany *(2035 figure has been estimated)*

Institutions need to keep an eye on jurisdiction and its implementation to make sure they remain sustainably and reliably functional[95]. If people's faith in this mechanism is destroyed (N. Luhmann, A. Peyrefitte[96], K. Röttgers), this will result in high transaction costs, which could lead the group to ruin – see the decline of Rome since Diocletian (284–305) and Constantine (306–337)[97]. Marxism and other totalitarian ideologies are examples of such aberrations.

The only alternative is the liberal, enlightened democracy within the framework of an – inevitable – globalisation if the human race as a whole is to be better off. A partitocracy needs the constitution to tame it. There is no way around utilitarian approaches if the problems are to be solved. The Catholic Social Doctrine adopts the same view and accordingly emphasises the two principles of efficiency and subsidiarity[98]. It is a strange fact that protestant churches, which evolved from the established church through the active intervention of princes, were never in a position to develop their own social doctrine which would go beyond the Ten Commandments.

Democracy – based on earlier draft constitutions (such as Venice in 466, Usages de Barcelona 1068, the Magna Carta 1215) and the election of a ruling elite, in an attempt to curb violence and murderous scenes like those depicted in Shakespeare's tragedies about royalty and nobility – is a dilemma which I would like to deal with at greater depth elsewhere. Aristotle (330 B.C.), Dante (1310 in "Monarchia" – on the Index of the Catholic Church), Schumpeter (1942), Dunn (1979, 2005) and Shapiro (2003) all expounded this topic. Dante echoed the views expressed by Aristotle, who branded this form of government "perverse" because it often led to mob rule (ochlocracy).

To my mind, the chances of a badly functioning democracy evolving to become a "world democracy" seem highly questionable in the light of the widely deviating interests of the different nations on the one hand and the absence of competition between the various models of state government on the other[99]. A hegemonial power like the USA appears to me to be the better concept of order provided it keeps an open ear for the concerns of the remaining 200 and more disparate states which, at best, would only be capable of creating a free trade zone within the framework of a European Union, for example.

But, as long as irresponsible lobbyists carve out advantages for just 2 per cent of the population – the commercial farmers and the Queen of England … – there can be no talk of justice. This also applies to the USA where the farming lobby, which similarly accounts for 2 per cent of the population, brought about the collapse of the Doha Round negotiations on the deregulation of world trade[100].

Accommodating the plurality of independent livelihoods and groups is what matters. These organisations, which are independent of the major nation – Hobbes' Leviathan, in other words – can range from the excellent doctor's surgery to small local firms of skilled tradesmen or service contractors, to global specialist companies and well-governed minor states like New Zealand, Australia, Singapore or Switzerland. What we need are role models that can initiate learning processes <u>under competition</u> and <u>without corruption</u> in order to promote universal well-being. Taxation is of secondary importance in this context, provided it doesn't stand in the way of the desired advancement of universal well-being. We need to experiment (H. Albert, K. Popper). In connection with the subject of universal well-being, we must also take a critical look at concepts that can only be described as ideologies as soon as they are handled in a dogmatic fashion:

- Democracy
- Equality
- Justice
- Dignity

The question of human rights and, above all – in the words of Küng – that of human responsibilities, ought to move us, and it might lead us to natural law[101,102]. Case-by-case justice falls outside the principle of a governmental administrative policy and remains a preserve of law courts, non-governmental organisations such as charities, including churches, as well as other NGOs. To this end, the State could support foundations more by subsidising them, as in the United States, for instance[103].

In view of the ratio of representation, democracies tend to create advantages for leaders skilled in the art of rhetoric and their political parties. I have already pointed out the negative consequences of partitocracy. While highly gifted individuals from industry, politics, science and art opt for inner emigration[104] or leave the country, people in leading positions, who are desperately needed by a community and are few and far between, are ousted, thus creating a void left by the skills and talent required to boost the national economy who have departed. This gives the administrative 'machine' more leverage – a circumstance expounded by Ellul, in particular – so the 'brain drain' becomes increasingly apparent, even to less perceptive observers[105 106,107].

The concepts of efficiency and subsidiarity, as employed in the Catholic Social Doctrine, are useful when it comes to demands made on the individual by the group. An individual can be expected to fulfil certain duties with the greatest possible efficiency in line with the latest technical advances, which should also correspond to the current state of knowledge. On no account should scarce resources be wasted. Every misallocation is to be avoided.

In a poignant article he published in 1997, H. Giersch drew attention to the antinomy between equality and prosperity[108]. This is a topic that is also covered by biosociology and sociobiology.[109]

If someone is unable to care for himself/herself, and especially if he or she relies on external help to meet his/her living costs, then that individual must do everything in his/her power to keep to a minimum the costs that the group, in this case, has to raise on his or her behalf. The group only provides support by helping the individual to help himself/herself. If this assistance is abused, it only serves to encourage subsistence.[110] The general standard of living should not play any role in these considerations. Earning one's living to the best of one's ability contributes towards a person's dignity. Surely this is self-evident?

What does this excursus on democracy (and inflation), efficiency and subsidiarity have to do with the topic in hand? To answer that question, we have to ask ourselves what happened in the year 1000. Why that particular year? It hinges on the aforementioned thesis by P. Bonnassie. The similarities to a developing country, such as Central Africa, and the situation in Catalonia prior to Islam, are startling.

3. The economy in Catalonia around 1000

3.1 Life in Catalonia

It was in 1000 that the first signs of an evolution, which we can now marvel at and hail as the Age of the Enlightenment and the medieval industrial revolution, appeared. Whatever the likes of Rousseau, Diderot, Voltaire, Kant and the inventors and industrialists achieved around the middle of the 18th century, the seeds were sown 700 years beforehand. There were several occurrences that subsequently hindered this development. The Hundred Years' War and the two Thirty Years' Wars were merely detail events. Religious ideologies were a cause of irrationality. We can draw comparisons with similar currents today. The recurring controversy surrounding P. C. Snow's "The Two Cultures" (1959) is proof of that; another example is the Catholic Church's irrational endeavours to reconcile religion and rationality[111]. The vestiges of the Frankfurt School and the pessimistic, naive sense of reality displayed by Bourdieu and Foucault, for example, also played a significant role in obstructing the progress that would make the world a better place to live in.[112]

In his book "The Forgotten Revolution", L. Russo describes circumstances in 1000 as follows:

"Links between science and technology, often claimed to have been non-existent before the modern age, are clear to Arab thinkers. Ibn Sina, or Avicenna (980–1037) lists the practical sciences that depend on geometry: geodesy, the science of automata, the kinematics of weights, the science of weights and balances, the

*science of measuring instruments, the science of lenses and mir-
rors, and the science of water transport.*"[113]

*"In the twelfth and thirteenth centuries the Iberian peninsula
and Sicily, taken back from Islam, and Southern Italy, which
had stayed in contact with Constantinople all along, were
important meeting points between European culture and the
scientific tradition that went back to Hellenistic times. In the
states arising from the Reconquista it was in fact possible to find
Hellenistic works and Arab scholars able to understand their
content, at least in part. Arabic translation of Euclid, Galen and
Ptolemy started to spread throughout Europe.*"[114]

I am fascinated by an English miniature depicting "God the
Builder" with scales, a pair of compasses and weighing and
measuring horns, which was crafted around 1050[115].

This is the framework for some of the socio-philosophical
problems that prevailed in Catalonia – between Christianity
and Islam – around 1000, during a period of considerable
change, which captured my interest and featured the following characteristics:

- legal certainty due to the West Gothic law
- increase in agricultural productivity
- bitter fighting over the distribution of profits
- influx of gold coins minted in Al-Andalus
- construction of 20 new monasteries during a building
  boom
- start of a substantial economic upswing

Catalonia is the small, north-eastern part of what was formerly
Roman Hispania. During the reign of Diocletian (284–305),

Hispania had a population of six million inhabitants[116]. Proud cities like Tarragona, Segovia, Cartagena and Barcelona belonged to the Roman province of Hispania. There are numerous aqueducts and other historical traces that date back to this era. Hispania was rich in mineral deposits, which were mined by the Romans before the dawn of the industrial age. Laietana wine from Barcelona was popular all over Europe.

The inner decline of the Roman Empire is a well-documented historical event, in which inflation played a major role. The siege of 100,000 Germanic barbarians from the north (some estimate the figure at 400,000) was only an outcome of Rome's inherent weakness. But the new Germanic rulers also fought relentlessly among themselves, thus playing into the hands of the Arabs and Berbers who managed to advance as far as Augustodunum in Gaul (now Autun in central France) in 711. Charlemagne protected his vast empire by waging war against the Arabs, a campaign that resulted in Catalonia being captured by the Franks, whereupon the Arabs colonised the region south of the Franconian March – Córdoba, Toledo, Tortosa and Granada – for seven centuries, a period that went down in history as a particularly turbulent era.

Catalonia was only sporadically affected by the culturally superior invaders. Following the fall of Barcelona, the Catalans settled high up in the Pyrenees in order to defend themselves against siege from the Saracens and Vikings. What was there to plunder from the subsistence farmers anyway? They were, however, free farmers to whom the Roman-West Gothic law applied until 1068 when it was replaced by the Catalan Magna Carta, the so-called "Usages de Barcelona", which marked the introduction of feudal law.

Fortified monasteries were built in the mountains in Pedro de la Roda, Ripoll, Urgel, Vic and other locations. Barcelona took a long time to recover from the decline of the Roman Empire.

There were only about one thousand inhabitants in the year 900. The siege of al-Mansur in 985 was another setback. Even in 1100, the rural city covered 30 hectares and had roughly 3,500 inhabitants: less than 100 m^2 per person. After that the population tripled every one hundred years and, by about 1300, numbered 30,000. The urban area occupied 120 hectares: the equivalent of 40 m^2 per inhabitant. Barcelona became the capital of a county/kingdom whose influence extended to the Balearic Islands, Sardinia and Sicily – and even as far as Athens.

To the south, the River Llobregat marked the border to the Arabian region – where Barcelona Airport is now situated. Tarragona, Tortosa and Lleida were under Islamic rule until 1128, 1148 and 1149 respectively. Following the Reconquista, this region became known as New Catalonia.

3.2 Modern Islam – ancient Christians

I will now proceed to address the short-lived economic realm of Old Catalonia, with a population of perhaps one million around the year 1000, and the developing capital city of Barcelona prior to the crusades. Modern Islam contradicted the ancient Christians. According to H. M. Enzensberger, it is the other way round nowadays.[117]

A comparison between West and East

G. Tate (1991) recounts what things were like on page 26 f. of "The Crusades and the Holy Land" (L'Orient des Croisades), translated by Lory Frankel:

"Compared with the East, the West seemed like a barbarous world; however, great changes were in the air. At the end of the 10th century the West was sparsely populated; its peasants were backward and oppressed. The best architecture it had to offer was castles made of wood; it had no money in circulation, waves of invaders had devastated the land, and its cultural life was restricted to the courts of princes and monasteries. The powers of authority were crumbling, and brutality held sway in social relations. After the year 1000 the large-scale invasions ceased and the population slowly began to expand. The peasants, armed now with better tools, cleared and enlarged the small parcels of land that they had reclaimed from the forest, and agricultural production increased. Using more productive farming methods, farmers created a surplus, which in turn encouraged trade. A steady and more abundant food source made famines and epidemics less frequent and severe. Cities began

to grow and set themselves off from the country. Even so, they could not compare to the rich metropolises of the East (the most populous among the western cities boasted no more than ten thousand inhabitants).

Westerners began making long voyages again, following the northern routes through Scandinavia and the Russian plains, crossing Central Europe and following the Danube River, and sailing the Mediterranean Sea from Italy and Catalonia. They exported raw materials and slaves and imported luxury goods. They could be found in the eastern ports, in Constantinople (present-day Istanbul), along the Syrian coast and in Alexandria."

This summarises the picture that the economic historian conjures up of Western Europe around the year 1000. There are already signs of globalisation, which was to expand during the eight crusades between 1096 and 1291. The scale of trade depends on prosperity and the amount of capital available. Transportation and transport routes play a considerable role.

The account begins with the arrival of the Christian Reconquista in the Iberian Peninsula, which had fallen into the hands of the Arabs in 711. Peace-loving Catalonia to the north-east of the peninsula was not so badly affected and, despite a number of setbacks such as the total destruction of Barcelona when troops from al-Mansur invaded in 985, attempted to capitalise on the borderland dividing the Christians from the Muslims. This situation is described in depth in P. Bonnassie's expansive treatise, which is outlined below.[118]

The abduction of Almodis by Jews and Arabs from Tortosa

A piquant story provides a telling insight into the good cooperation between Christians, Jews and Muslims, as well as the emancipation of women who occupied a prominent position at the Catalan court[119].

Here is the plot in brief:

Raimund (Ramón) Berenguer I, the young Count of Barcelona, made the acquaintance of the 30-year-old Almodis de la Marca, the Countess of Toulouse, in Narbonne on a pilgrimage to Rome. She already had four children from her second marriage (in 1040) to Count Pons of Toulouse. In 1052, in a flagrant breach of all established morals and customs, he entrusted some Jewish merchants with the task of kidnapping Almodis, which they accomplished with the aid of an Islamic fleet sent from Tortosa. The sea voyage across the Golfe du Lion and maybe even as far as Italy was entirely under Islamic control, even if Jewish merchants were in charge of the operation. The wedding was held in the new Romanesque cathedral of Barcelona immediately after Almodis' abduction, despite the fact that both bride and groom were still married to their former spouses. Twins were born in 1053. Pope Victor II excommunicated both bigamists three times in succession for this illegal marriage. In Catalonia, Countess Ermessenda roused the barons to stage a rebellion. The Count of Besalú was not to be pacified – not even by the prospect of marrying Almodis' sister. The newlyweds were accused of unnecessarily and inadvisably sabotaging the social function of marriage. The moral code was being thrown overboard and family interests betrayed for the sake of an amorous liaison. The political affiliation with Rome, which had been nurtured for 50 years, was under threat. Following the wedding, the nobles were required to swear two oaths of allegiance. It appears that, on the whole, their marriage had quite a favourable impact. Clear evidence of Almodis' influence on jurisdiction is provided in the "Usages de Barcelona"[120].

This marriage serves as an example of Catalonia's affinity to France (Languedoc) in the north rather than to Spain (León) in the west. People were not averse to taking advantage of Jews and Arabs, however, when love was involved. The scandalous story was made into a French film in 2004.[121]

We may wonder how they managed to avoid a clash of cultures. What are the prerogatives for a harmonious coexistence between the three Abrahamic, monotheistic religions: Jews, Christians and Muslims? It is likely that trade and the prospects of reciprocal advantages were conducive to maintaining peace.

3.3 The blossoming of finance

Economic development between 980 and 1050 was funda-
mentally rooted in the continual influx of Muslim gold. Barcelona became the Eldorado of the West, a circumstance that
only seems possible, however, because agricultural innovations led to a farming surplus that could be bought and sold
at the market. This called for money – coupled with a reason
for earning money, i.e. goods on which to spend it. All this
coincided with a flourishing economy largely due to the trade
relations with the Muslim neighbours. Not even al-Mansur's
invasion of Barcelona was able to halt this development.

The Gold Rush

As from 970, small quantities of Arabian currency including
gold coins (mancusos) came into circulation in Catalonia.
Following the siege of Barcelona by a raiding force under
al-Mansur in 985, circulation increased progressively, creating a kind of gold fever among the contemporary population. Around 965, Córdoba gradually gained control of the
gold routes through the Sahara. Minting was concentrated
in North Africa and Córdoba, and coins even travelled as far
away as Barcelona. From 1018 onwards, the rich Jew Bonhom
started minting the first gold coins in Barcelona under the
supervision of Countess Ermessenda. To begin with, they
were identical to the Arabian coins. Christian coins were em-
bossed with Allah, the Islamic god.

Islamic gold coins also appeared in Castile and León, although they did not count as legal tender as they were used

for military purposes to fund the battles they waged. In Catalonia, however, they remained a popular means of currency, particular for property transactions, until 1050. The coins were differentiated according to their provenance. The euphoria for gold changed from about 1020. This was due to the practice of hoarding gold and a reduction in gold imports.

Only a small number of people hoarded gold for investment purposes as a means of generating revenue. For the majority of the population, gold did not serve any purpose in its own right, so the velocity of circulation must have been fairly high. The precious metal was, however, also used for jewellery and for adorning churches, such as the treasure belonging to the cathedral of Girona. But hoarding alone cannot account for the decline in monetary transactions. Due to the collapse of Córdoba, it was unable to maintain its influence on North Africa, so the flow of gold waned. The political situation in Barcelona made matters worse. The introduction of Arabian gold coins was accompanied by the first credits granted on provision of a collateral in 970, which became much more widespread during the first half of the 11th century. Loans were kept on a small scale; interest rates needed to correspond to the degree of risk involved.

Gothic law, which was still in force at the time, did not prohibit extortion, so credit negotiations were conducted publicly. The most common form of credit was short-term, i.e. less than one year. If the debtor failed to pay back the loan, it was only possible to liquidate the collaterals deposited by means of a procedure known as the Code of Réceswinth in conjunction with the judgement pronounced by three "boni homines".

Inflation was also a problem: prices for vineyards increased fivefold in and around Barcelona between 970 and 1050, within the space of 80 years, in other words. There was apparently more money available than merchandise on which to spend it, and this led to the price increases.

3.4 The ups and downs of foreign trade

We know from documents and archaeological finds, such as coins, jewellery, items of everyday use, etc. that trading routes crossed the Pyrenees through the mountain passes of Perthus, where there was shelter, and Cerdagne. Expensive luxury goods from Al-Andalus were probably shipped to Toulouse. In return, they purchased fabrics that were not available in Catalonia. Materials were mainly imported via Paris, but also from Flanders. There is evidence to show that a merchant from Flanders called Robert stayed in Barcelona in 1009.

Sourcing evidence is far from simple. There are very few signs of trading. There again, why should merchants want to leave any traces that might well incur high taxes and duties? It is not wise to flaunt one's wealth. Jews have repeatedly suffered as a result.

During the first half of the 11th century, the excellent relations between the Counts of Barcelona and their Islamic neighbours fostered direct trade. A document dated 1011 provides evidence of coastal shipping. Roads were also used for transportation: the *strata francisca* was renamed the *strata morischa* with effect from 1046. We know from the testaments that mainly textiles (cotton, wool, camel hair, silk and brocade), artefacts made of gold and silver, as well as spices were imported. Around 1010, it became fashionable for noblemen and noblewomen to wear silken robes. Even rich farmers passed on silk belts to their heirs. Most items were manufactured in Andalusia, but occasionally some came from North Africa and even as far afield as Syria.

How were imported goods paid for?

There is documentary evidence to show which means of payment were used for this merchandise, if we put aside the production of arms in the Pyrenees. Judging by expeditions to Córdoba in 1010–1020 it is estimated that the amount of gold coins in circulation in Catalonia amounted to more than 3,000 mancusos. We have to assume that the Catalonian mercenary soldiers who served the Arabs brought the gold treasure into the country, thus strengthening the economy. Catalonia exported its main resource – people. Arabian tributes were only paid after Al-Andalus collapsed and split up into a number of taifa kingdoms, which then boosted prosperity.

4. What happened next? – Looking ahead

After the conquest of Mallorca (in 1229), the new kingdom became a kind of high-medieval Dubai, if we follow M. Borgolte's drift:

"The island was mainly inhabited by Catalans, but also by people of Provençal and Italian origin, and the ruler expressly encouraged Jews from Spain, Languedoc and North Africa to settle there, so it gradually forfeited its Islamic identity. It was now possible to conduct trade (…) with North African sultanates and cities (Ceuta, Oran, Algiers, Bougie, Tlemçen, Tunis, etc.) from Barcelona via Mallorca. In the Valencian realm, King Jaume granted the vanquished Muslim population local self-administration and the freedom to exercise their religious beliefs. (…) It was only towards the end of the 14th century that Christians made up the majority of the population."

D. Abulafia wrote the following account of the period:

"The city of Valencia paid revenue to the Crown from Muslim bathhouses, bakeries, slaughterhouses and brothels, as well as poll taxes from Muslims and Jews and fees from market and dock trade (…). It was a community full of contradictions, however: differences between the conquerors and the conquered; between Muslims who spoke Arabic and Christians who made use of Catalan; between Gothic church spires and Islamic minarets; between clean-shaven Christians who ate pork and bearded Jews and Muslims who abided by the traditional food regulations."

Catastrophe struck in 1492 when the Spanish monarchy wantonly expelled the Muslims and Jews, a catastrophe from which Spain was only to recover 500 years later when it joined the European Union following the death of Franco. From this year on, Toledo became a cultural wasteland.

Lasting influences: numerals – loanwords

What is left? It was the Arabic numerals that first stimulated the rise of modern scientific thought. Arabic loanwords were assimilated into Spanish and Catalan, just as they became a common feature of the English language, for instance:

admiral	alchemy	arsenal	borax
fakir	hazard	hashish	cable
coffee	calibre	lacquer	mosque
risk	cheque	syrup	sugar

Of equal importance is the influence exerted by the Koran on the principles of predetermination, which narrows down a person's free will and accordingly his or her level of responsibility.

It may be possible to solve the dilemma between religion and rationality.[122] Two remarkable philosophers, both of whom were born in Córdoba – Maimonides (a Jew, 1135–1204) and Averroes (a Muslim, 1126–1198) – believed in rationality, which to their minds embodied something godlike. That was a new approach. They were opposed to believing in miracles and instead pinned their hopes on clarity of thought, arguing that faith was the only way to know God's kingdom. Both were expelled, lived in exile in North Africa and ended up as personal physicians in the service of Islamic rulers: Maimonides at the court of Saladin in Fustet near Cairo, Averroes at the Moroccan court in Marrakesh. Both symbolised an attempt at medieval enlightenment which, it seems, failed to get through to the population, even if there are reports of scepticism[123]. Habermas[124], Albert[125] and Schnädelbach[126] are of relevance in this connection.

Looking ahead: Globalisation today is far more intense because of the huge rise in prosperity, which fuels the demand for foreign goods, due to increased productivity which results from technical advancement. Distance is no longer an issue, for communications and the cost of sending or transporting goods has become so much cheaper that it is worth employing pay differentials to economic advantage. In a speech given on 25 August 2006, Ben Bernanke, Chairman of the Federal Reserve, the central bank of the United States, and Professor of Economics[127] at Princeton University, warned that:

"The current 'unprecedented' pace of global economic integration could raise living standards and cut poverty, but those benefits are at risk from geopolitical tensions and protectionism. Economic and technological changes are likely to shrink effective distances still further in coming years, creating the potential for continued improvements in productivity and living standards and for a reduction in global poverty. The challenge for policymakers is to ensure that the benefits of global economic integration are sufficiently widely shared. (…)

The process of global economic integration has been going on for thousands of years, and the sources and consequences of this integration have often borne at least a qualitative resemblance to those associated with the current episode. Two thousand years ago, the Romans unified their far-flung empire through an extensive transportation network and a common language, legal system and currency."

In those days, there were only very few people who could afford luxuries, but food imports were always a high priority, especially in the face of famine.

"In recent years, global merchandise exports have been above 20 per cent of world gross domestic product, compared with about 8 per cent in 1913. (...) Displaced workers [should] get the necessary training to take advantage of new opportunities (...)"

The fast pace of globalisation must not disguise the fact that poor subsistence farmers and the unemployed can hardly contribute anything towards economic growth. Only growing prosperity and the accumulation of capital – especially among mid-tier entrepreneurs – leads to globalisation and – coupled with increased productivity due to technical and organisational innovations – to a decline in costs. If they are given instruction in more advanced working techniques and have access to small loans (microfinance), subsistence farmers can work much more efficiently and attain a surplus that enables them to share in the generally higher living standards[128].

The development of the monetary system and trade in Catalonia around the year 1000, as dealt with in this essay, serves as an example of economic growth. At the same time, the give and take between Christians and Muslims on the Iberian Peninsula also illustrates how conflicting intercultural values, which are a cause for concern in a relatively small country like Germany with its high rate of demographic loss, and where five per cent of the population is of Islamic origin, might possibly be offset. But, as M. Borgolte concludes in his book about Christians, Jews and Moors:

"The successful integration of Greek and Arabian science and philosophy (...) simultaneously paved the way and provided the impetus for the de-christianisation of Europe."

This included the monetary system and simplifications in the conduct of trade that accompanied it. To what extent the church itself contributed to its own demise through irrational behaviour – such as the corruption of historical facts through countless biographies of St. Francis of Assizi or the prohibition of thought, as laid down in 219 articles in Paris in 1277, to quote just two examples[129] – shall be reserved for a separate investigation.

Karen Horn – president of the Hayek Society – looks into the role and responsibilities of economics and poses a number of questions, which I would like to use to conclude this essay[130]:

"It is the major issues, the socio-philosophical aspects that need to be reinstated when it is a question of keeping in touch with reality:

How do societies learn?

How does the creative process, in which dispersed existing knowledge is collated and then interwoven and multiplied through the interaction of various individuals, work without these people actually realising it?

How do collective religious systems, standards and mentalities develop?

How are formal and informal institutions formed?

Which ones are beneficial for economic development?

… trade relations and human interaction – it is precisely with this in mind that they invented the institution of 'the market'."

5. Literature

J. Attali: "Les Juifs, le Monde et l'Argent", Paris 2002 ["The Economic History of the Jewish People", 2009]

L. Benevolo: "Die Stadt in der europäischen Geschichte", Munich 1999

P. Bezbakh: "Histoire de Économie – Des Origines à la Mondialisation", Paris 2005

P. Bonnassie: "La Catalogne au Tournant de l'An Mil", Paris 1990

M. Borgolte: "Europa entdeckt seine Vielfalt 1050–1250", Stuttgart 2002

J. M. Broekman: "Recht und Anthropologie", Freiburg 1979

B. Catlos: "The Victors and the Vanquished. Christians and Muslims of Catalonia and Aragon 1050–1300", 2004

H. F. Cohen and T. E. Huff: "Why the West", Seminar Alpbach 2005

P. Contamine et al. "L'Économie medieval", 3rd edition, Paris 2003

W. Dalrymple: "Return to Xanadu – The world today is not so different from the way it was in Marco Polo's time", Time 07.08.2006

L. Feuchtwanger: "Die Jüdin von Toledo", Hamburg 1955

J. Fourastié: "Le grand espoir du XXe siècle", Paris 1947, 1963

M. Gargalo: "Les disculpas del islam", La Vanguardia 28.09.2006

J. Gimpel: "La Révolution Industrielle du Moyen Age", Paris 1975

D. S. Landes: "The Wealth and Poverty of Nations – Why some are so rich and some are so poor", New York 1998

M. North (ed.): "Deutsche Wirtschaftsgeschichte", Munich 2000

J. Pfeffer and R. I. Sutton: "The Knowing-Doing Gap – How Smart Companies Turn Knowledge into Action", Boston 1999

J. J. Piderit: "Ethical Foundations of Economics", Washington 1993

A. Rucquoi: "Histoire médiévale de la péninsule ibérique", Paris 1993

M. Sancho i Planas: "Catalunya any zero – El paper de l'islam en els nostres origins", Barcelona 2005

B. Schefold (ed.): "Über N. Oresmius' 'Tractatus de Moneta' – Vademecum zu einem Klassiker der mittelalterlichen Geldlehre", Düsseldorf 1995

M. Schmoeckel: "Auf der Suche nach der verlorenen Ordnung – 2.000 Jahre Recht in Europa – Ein Überblick", Cologne 2005

F. Seibt: "Die Begründung Europas", 4th edition, Frankfurt 2003

H. de Soto: "Freiheit für das Kapital – Warum der Kapitalismus nicht weltweit funktioniert", preface by L. Spät, Berlin 2002

G. Spendel: "Für Vernunft und Recht", Tübingen 2004

J. Valdeón Baruque: "La Reconquista – El Concepto de España: Unidad y Diversidad", Madrid 2006

6. Annexes

6.1 Historical dates: from the Arabs to the Reconquista

Arabs and Berbers in Hispania	711
Cardona Castle	**798**
Wilfredo "the Hairy"	879–897
Ripoll Monastery	879
Borrell II (Count of Barcelona)	947–992
Ermessenda de Carcassona	972–1057
Plundering by al-Mansur	985
Franconia's independence	988
Ramón Borrell	988–1017
Abbot Oliva of Ripoll	1008–1046
(Catalan) Scriptorium with 200 translations	
Visit from Gerbert of Aurillac (later Pope Sylvester II)	
Berenguer Ramón I.	1018–1035
Almodis de la Marca	**1020–1071**
Ramón Berenguer I, the Elder	**1035–1076**
Romanesque cathedrals	1046–1058
Population of 20,000	
New Catalonia	1128–1149
Saladin (Muslim general)	1138–1193

6.2 Eminent sons of merchants and noblemen

Augustine	354–430
Benedict of Nursia	480–553
Mohammed	570–632
Bernard of Clairvaux	1090–1153
Thomas à Becket	1118–1170
Averroes (Ibn Rushd)	1126–1192
Maimonides	1135–1204
Francis of Assisi	1181–1226
Roger Bacon	1220–1292
Thomas Aquinas	1225–1274

6.3 Development of world population

Whenever we look at a detailed description – about life in Catalonia around the year 1000, for instance – it is vital that we don't lose sight of the broader historical picture. This certainly includes demographic development, which has repeatedly given cause for concern, especially since the days of the English economist Malthus (1766–1884). His remarks about the "struggle for existence" provided the key to Darwin's (1809–1882) natural selection theory.

As we can see from the table below, the world around the turn of the second millennium, with its population of 320 million people, was sparsely inhabited compared with today's global population of more than 6.5 billion. There were 6 million people altogether on the Iberian Peninsula, roughly 1 million of whom lived in Catalonia.

It took 900 years for this figure to double. Since then, the number of people in the world has increased 20-fold and the time it has taken for this figure to double has dropped to one-twentieth or less than 50 years. Changes like this must inevitably have consequences for people's mentality as well as their intellectual and technical faculties, because they have to find a means of survival. So innovations were called for. Superstitions had to disappear in order to avoid economic disaster, but I do not intend to elaborate on these matters at this point.

Table 1: Development of world population[131]

P	Year	Population	Doubled in
1	7000	10 million	
2	4500	20 million	2,500 years
3	2500	40 million	2,000 years
4	1000	80 million	1,500 years
5	0	160 million	1,000 years
6	900	320 million	900 years
7	1700	600 million	800 years
8	1850	1,200 million	150 years
9	1950	2,500 million	100 years
10	1986	5,000 million	36 years
11	2012	7,000 million	70 years (?)

Nobody embodies the different aspects of Jewish fate in the midst of this brilliant and fairly tolerant Islam better than Moses Maimonides, a rabbi, physician and court councillor. Born in Córdoba in 1135, he was 13 when the Almohades invaded the city and prohibited the Jewish community from practising their faith. His family pretended to convert to Islam but emigrated at the same time to Morocco, some distance away from the Almohad dynasty, where they met up with numerous freedom-seeking intellectuals again: Muslims – such as Averroes (Ibn Rushd), the famous commentator on Aristotle, who had flown to Marrakesh – and Jews alike, most of the latter having settled in Fez. Moses Maimonides studied the Talmud and both Greek and Islamic philosophers more or less in secret (he was later to write the words: "There is no purer monotheism than Islam"). He was 22 years old when he wrote a textbook about the calendar.

In 1165 the Almohades tightened their grip on Morocco; even practising the Jewish faith clandestinely became very dangerous. But peace reigned in Egypt and Maimonides moved to Alexandria, a decaying city, in about 1165 (according to Benjamin of Tudela, there were only 3,000 Jews left in 1177). He was reunited with his brother who had settled there shortly before him in the hope of making his fortune by trading with the countries of the Indian Ocean. But his brother drowned in the Red Sea in 1169. Maimonides, who was by now a young man with a considerable inheritance, married and moved to Fustat, a suburb of Cairo, where most of the city's Jewish community dwelt. He devoted his time to the twin practices of theology and medicine.

In 1185, he became personal physician to the vizier al Fadil, Saladin's successor when he departed for Damascus (1138–1193).

He received rabbis and Islamic scholars who were avidly studying Greek mathematics and Egyptian science. It was in this milieu of intellectuals and educated merchants, who were intrigued by the clash between the Koran and Aristotle, that he undertook to prove – in Arabic – that Jewish philosophy provides a sensible explanation for human existence. He wrote his "Guide for the perplexed" in about 1190, going beyond the "Book of the Fathers" and the arguments put forward by the rabbi Hillel by updating and aligning them to the Greek and Islamic universe. He attempted to reconcile collective and individual interests, belief and rationality, the Bible and Aristotle – coinciding almost exactly with Averroes' philosophical writings on behalf of Islam. To Maimonides' mind, everyone was free to live according to his beliefs and interpretations ("Only the Torah can call itself holy: all other laws are the work of humankind"). In the circle of merchants and travellers, in which he moved, he placed emphasis on taking personal responsibility. He even went as far as deducing that the best form of charity was to help the poor "with gifts – in the form of either loans or active support – to set up their own livelihood so they no longer need to seek help". In other words, it is only possible to overcome poverty if the rich finance the projects of the poor.

Creative work is the only decent way to accumulate wealth. And everyone who has the means is morally obliged to lend money to non-Jews under the proviso that they don't charge excessive interest and only make loans to women to enable them to avoid (financial) dependence.

When Maimonides died in 1204, his children formed a dynasty of rabbis and community leaders who dominated the Egyptian Jews until the country was conquered by the Ottoman Turks in 1517. This dynasty went back to the father-in-law of one of his sons, the rabbi Abraham Hananael who, as the wealthy owner of a sugar refinery, was simultaneously responsible for all the rabbinical courts in Egypt. Their task was to arbitrate in conflicts between the merchants who were in India or China in search of spices and silk respectively, in order to sell these goods in Europe.

Before long, Maimonides' work became well known in the Jewish communities in Islamic and Christian countries: his books accompanied merchants on their journeys. They influenced the earliest beginnings of the ethics of rational individualism in Western Christian countries – commencing in Egypt. Maimonides took this opportunity to define the concepts of individual mercy and the immortality of the soul, which influenced Thomas Aquinas, and the values of freedom and responsibility, which led to the ethics of capitalism. Many people who subsequently claimed to be contemplating the origins of modernity were to forget these Jewish-Islamic sources: Hillel, Averroes and Maimonides.

6.5 God the Builder of the Universe (1050)[133]

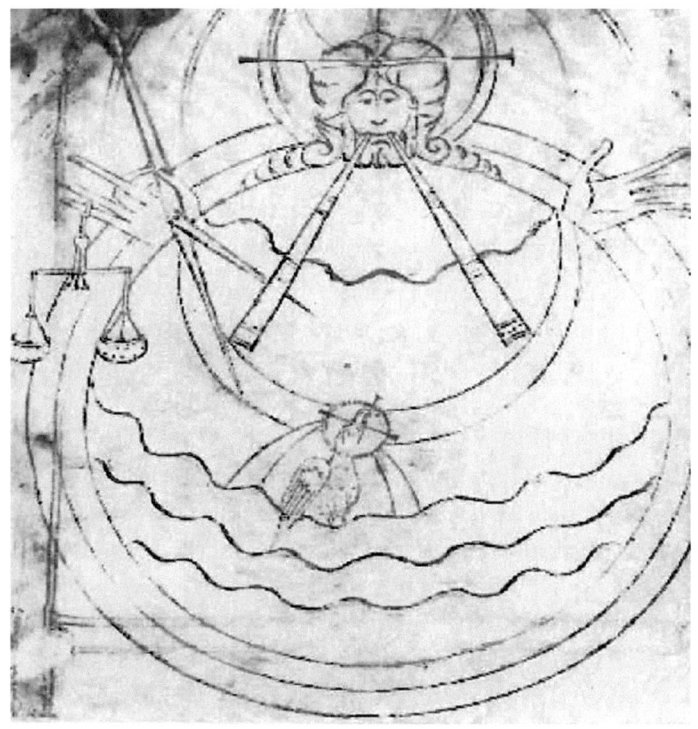

Fig. 4: God, the Builder (1050)

About the author

Name
Dr. Peter Seidler, Dipl.-Chem., born on 23th November 1936 in Hamburg (Germany).

Career
Former managing partner of astradur Industrieboden AG (retired in 2009).

Core business areas
High-performance polymers for coating and repairing industrial floors: polymer-impregnated concrete, protective coatings for concrete surfaces and polymer-concrete overlays.

Author's profile
After A-levels (1955) in Hamburg, he studied chemistry and physics at the Universities of Karlsruhe (now Karlsruhe Institute of Technology – KIT), Lausanne and the Sorbonne (on a French government scholarship), completing his doctoral thesis on a NATO scholarship at the CNRS national research institute in Paris under the direction of A. Chapiro. The subject of his thesis was acrylic acid grafting copolymerisation onto the surface of PTFE film using cobalt 60-y radiation to improve the adhesion properties.

Studies in business administration at INSEAD in Fontainebleau (France).

From 1963 onwards he specialised in the adhesion of building materials and high-performance polymers for heavy-duty industrial floors. His main fields of interest include:

benchmarking (a European Eureka project), knowledge management, workflow optimisation and the industrialisation of the building trade.

Numerous publications. Editor of the industrial floors manual "Handbuch Industrieböden", 4th edition, "Kunststoffe auf der Baustelle" (Plastics on the building site) and CD-ROM "Industrieböden" (Industrial floors). 1987–2007 initiator and scientific coordinator of the international colloquia on industrial floors at the Technische Akademie Esslingen (TAE). Chairman of RILEM TC 184 "Industrial Floors". Board member of ICPIC – International Congress on Polymers in Concrete. Talks given in San Francisco (USA), Bahia (Brazil), Ostend (Belgium), Bled (Slovenia), Bologna (Italy), San Antonio (USA), Kruger Park (South Africa), Honolulu (USA) and Dundee (UK). Member of GDCh expert group "Building Chemistry" and ICRI.

Joint recipient of the Owen Nutt Award, in conjunction with L. Czarnecki (TU Warsaw), at the 11th International Congress on Polymers in Concrete in 2004 held at the Federal Institute for Materials Research and Testing (BAM) in Berlin.

Philosophy of Economics under Prof. K. Röttgers at Fern-Universität Hagen.

List of illustrations

Notes

Part I

[1] M. Reder and J. Schmidt (ed.): "Ein Bewusstsein von dem, was fehlt – Eine Diskussion mit Jürgen Habermas", Frankfurt 2008.

[2] Frankfurter Allgemeine newspaper (FAZ) dated 24.01.2007.

[3] Source: R. Metz, Säkulare Trends der deutschen Wirtschaft, in M. North (ed.): "Deutsche Wirtschaftsgeschichte – Ein Jahrtausend im Überblick" (German Economic History), p. 426, Munich 2000.

[4] The English/French word "serf" is derived from the Latin "servus" meaning a slave.

[5] See H. de Soto: "Freiheit für das Kapital", Berlin 2002.

[6] Quoted from E. Bahr (ed.) "Was ist Aufklärung? – Thesen und Definitionen", Stuttgart 1974, p. 9; I. Kant: "Answering the question: What is Enlightenment?" (1784).

[7] Source: Duby 1991, quoted from K.-H. Ludwig's Technik im hohen Mittelalter zwischen 1000 und 1350/1400, in W. König (ed.): "Propyläen Technikgeschichte", Vol. 2, p. 18, Berlin 1992.

[8] F. Crouzet: "Histoire de l'Économie Européenne 1000–2000" (A history of the European Economy), Paris 2000.

[9] M. Brater and C. Munz: "Die pädagogische Bedeutung der Buchführung – Überlegungen und Erfahrungen zu ihrem Einsatz in der Waldorfschule" (On the educational value of book-keeping – thoughts and experience regarding its use in Rudolf Steiner schools), Stuttgart 1994.

[10] F. Crouzet, ibid.

[11] M. Bloch: "Esquisse d'une Histoire Monétaire de l'Europe", Paris 1954, quoted in F. Crouzet, p. 67.

[12] M. Bu: "Suger – Abbé de Saint-Denis – Régent de France", Paris 1991.

[13] P. Charles-Dominique: "Voyageurs Arabes", Paris 1998.

[14] K. Röttgers and P. Koslowski (ed.): "Transkulturelle Wertekonflikte – Theorie und wirtschaftsethische Praxis", Heidelberg 2002.

[15] P. Sloterdijk: "Falls Europa erwacht. Gedanken zum Programm einer Weltmacht am Ende des Zeitalters ihrer politischen Absence", Frankfurt 1994.

[16] A. Schuller: "Wir brauchen das Imperium Americanum" – FAZ 09.03.2003, p. 11. This is also discussed in detail by Niall Ferguson in: "Das verleugnete Imperium – Chancen und Risiken amerikanischer Macht", Berlin 2004 ("Colossos – The Rise and Fall of the American Empire" London 2004).

[17]   Quoted from J. Meran: "Wirtschaftsphilosophie – Teil 1 Wirtschafts-
       ethik" (The Philosophy of Economics – Part I Business Ethics), p. 19.
[18]   L. Strauss: "Xenophon's Socratic Discourse – An Interpretation of
       the Oeconomicus", South Bend 1998.
[19]   cf. A. Abdel-Malek in F. Châtelet: "La Philosophie Médiévale",
       pp. 145–168; "Ibn Khaldoûn Fondateur de la Science Historique et
       de la Sociologie".
[20]   Collated from various English translations of Ibn Khaldun's al-
       Muqaddimah (Prolegomena, or Introduction to History).
[21]   Quoted from R. Dunbar: "The Trouble with Science", London 1995,
       p. 96.
[22]   Ibid, p. 96.
[23]   Ibid, p. 102.
[24]   Le Petit Robert.
[25]   Le Petit Robert.
[26]   Piderit, pp. 119–120.
[27]   Piderit, p. 124.
[28]   Merchants from Amalfi were killed in Cairo in 996.
[29]   See W. Shakespeare: "The Merchant of Venice".
[30]   R. Gaettens: "Geschichte der Inflationen – Vom Altertum bis zur
       Gegenwart", Munich 1982, p. 40.
[31]   SHMES: "L'Argent au Moyen Age", conference proceedings, Paris
       1998.
[32]   S. Jenks, in M. North (ed.): "Deutsche Wirtschaftsgeschichte" (Ger-
       man Economic History), 2000, p. 29.
[33]   Quoted from Büchner's "Leonce and Lena".
[34]   Piderit, p. 118.
[35]   Quoted from K. Popper: "Open Society and its Enemies" I and II,
       5th edition, p. 398.
[36]   Quoted from J. Meran: "Wirtschaftsphilosophie – Teil 1 Wirtschafts-
       ethik" (The Philosophy of Economics – Part I Business Ethics), p. 73.
[37]   See Part 2.
[38]   See Part 3.
[39]   FAZ 07.02.2004, p. 41.

Part II.

[40]   cf. Annex 3.
[41]   cf. D. S. Landes in the Annex.
[42]   cf. A. Comte in the Annex.
[43]   The premium for scrapping old cars, introduced in the autumn of
       2009 to boost election chances, is a good example.
[44]   See P. Kirchhoff, FAZ 28.05.2009.

45 "The state should be a constitutional state; that is the key; in fact, it is also the stimulus needed for development at any one time. Apart from determining and anchoring the course and limitations of its authority, such as the scope of liberty accorded to its citizens, precisely and irrefutably within the provisions of the law, it should also refrain from implementing (enforcing) the official moral concepts imposed by the government (directly, in other words) any further than is required by the statutes, i.e. only as far as is legally indispensable." (F. J. Stahl, 1856, quoted in M. Schmoeckel).

46 REACH stands for Registration, Evaluation and Authorisation of Chemical Products.

47 Hans Böckler Foundation of the Federation of German Trade Unions – Institute for Macro Economics and Business Research (IMK) – Academic Director.

48 See P. Sloterdijk: "Im selben Boot – Versuch über die Hyperpolitik", Frankfurt 1995, p. 54 ff.

49 Gottfried Seebass: "Moralische Verantwortung", in Zeitschrift für philosophische Forschung, 48, H. 2 (1994).

50 cf. M. Reddé & J.-C. Colvin: "Voyages sur la Méditerranée Romaine", Paris 2005, p. 7.

51 cf. P. Niesen: "Kants Theorie der Redefreiheit", Baden-Baden 2005; reviewed by W. Kersting, FAZ 14.09.2005.

52 The Concise Oxford Dictionary (4th ed.): Epistemology, Theory of the method or grounds of knowledge (f. Gk *episteme* knowledge).

53 cf. Chapter entitled "The Logical Mind", in R. Dunbar: "The Trouble with Science", pp. 108–113.

54 W. Lippmann pointed this out in 1927 in "The Phantom Public".

55 'Patronage' on the part of the state can achieve much less in this case.

56 See R. Sennett: "The Craftsman", Yale University Press, 2008 and M. B. Crawford: "Shop Class as Soulcraft – An Inquiry into the Value of Work", London 2009.

57 This chapter is taken from my first essay, in which I already addressed this issue.

58 Merchants from Amalfi were killed in Cairo in 996.

59 H. Trofimoff: "L'assurance contra la fortune de mer en France", in A. Corbin & H. Richard (ed.): "La Mer – Terreur et Fascination", Paris 2004, pp. 93–95.

60 F. Crouzet, ibid.

61 M. Bloch: "Esquisse d'une Histoire Monétaire de l'Europe", Paris 1954, quoted in F. Crouzet, p. 67.

62   R. Gaettens: "Geschichte der Inflationen – Vom Altertum bis zur Gegenwart", Munich 1982, p. 40.

63   S.H.M.E.S.: "L'Argent au Moyen Age", conference proceedings, Paris 1998.

64   S. Jenks in M. North (ed.): "Deutsche Wirtschaftsgeschichte" (German Economic History), 2000, p. 29.

65   Quoted from P. Contamine et al.: "L'économie medieval", 3rd edition, Paris 2003, p. 383.

66   Picot and Reichwald 1991, p. 276, quoted in Romeike/Finke.

67   H. de Soto: "The Mystery of Capital: Why Capitalism Triumphs in the West and Fails Everywhere Else".

68   "Auf der Suche nach der verlorenen Ordnung – 2000 Jahre Recht in Europa" (2005).

69   FAZ 21.09.2005.

70   All patents are granted for a term of 20 years; other intellectual property (literature …) is protected by copyright for the author's lifetime plus 50…70 years.

71   cf. Annex 4.

72   A. MacIntyre: "After Virtue", pp. 128–139 (1981); N. N. Taleb provides a summary in: "Fooled by Randomness – The Hidden Role of Chance in Life and in the Markets", 2nd ed. London 2004.

73   FAZ 06.11.2005, p. 43.

74   Rheinpfalz 07.11.2005.

75   Arthur Conte: "Les paysans de France de l'an 1000 à l'an 2000", Plan 2000, pp. 173–174.

76   It was only in the 21st century that the emphasis shifted from "agriculture" to "services" etc.

77   Excerpt from David S. Landes: "The Wealth and Poverty of Nations – Why Some Are So Rich and Some So Poor", New York 1998. (Chapter entitled: "Loss of Leadership")

78   U. Beck: "Risk Society" (1986), Chapter VII Science beyond Truth and Enlightenment? Reflexivity and critique of techno-scientific progress, pp. 256–257.

79   Excerpt from an article written by RA E. Caspary, FSZ 09.10.05.

Part III

80   The section on establishing the social market economy is intentionally detailed to provide material for a proposed expansion on the treatise. The essay accordingly consists of two parts: "Justification for the social market economy" and "The economy in Catalonia around 1000".

[81] Talk given at the Römerbad-Tage, Badenweiler, "Von der Beweglichkeit des Politikers" (On the politician's mobility), 04.02.1994.

[82] Quoted from B. Bueb, in "Die Macht der Eltern – Vom richtigen Gebrauch der Autorität in Erziehungsfragen" (Parental power – on the right use of authority in children's upbringing), FAZ 14.09.2006.

[83] cf. G. Soros: "De Karl Popper a Karl Rove", La Vanguardia 15.11.2007, p. 28.

[84] See K. Acham (ed.): "Moral und Kunst im Zeitalter der Globalisierung", Vienna 2002; J. Bagwhati: "In Defense of Globalisation", Oxford 2004; B. Guillochon: "La Mondialisation – Une seule planète, des projets divergents", Paris 2004; J. E. Stiglitz: "Making Globalisation Work", New York 2006; M. Wolf: "Why Globalization Works", New Haven 2004. The current financial crisis is due solely to gross governmental incompetence, as Taylor and others have shown. Early warnings, such as those sounded by M. Wolf, were ignored.

[85] P. Cahuc, F. Kramarz and A. Zylberberg: "Les ennemis de la concurrence et de l'emploi", Commentary No. 114, summer 2006.

[86] G. Radnitzky: Acceptance speech on being awarded the 2004 Arthur Koestler Prize in Augsburg.

[87] See Ludwig Erhard, Nell-Breuning and Piderit.

[88] See G. Ifrah: "Universalgeschichte der Zahlen", Frankfurt 1993.

[89] I have not come across any remarks on this subject in existing literature so far.

[90] cf. W. Hegel, Vol. 7, p. 492.

[91] cf. W. Hegel, Vol. 3, p. 354.

[92] M. Friedman: "Dollars and Deficits", New Jersey 1968.

[93] FAZ 04.09.2006.

[94] IWF lt. http://de.wikipedia.org/wiki/inflation.

[95] See J. Buchanan, 1962.

[96] A. Peyrefitte: "La société de confiance", Paris 1995 – state doctoral thesis (thèse d'État).

[97] See M. Rostovtzeff: "Geschichte der Alten Welt – Rom", Bremen 1970, among other works.

[98] See Nell-Breuning, Küng, Piderit. This matter is addressed in the first essay.

[99] See I. Kant: "Zum ewigen Frieden" (On eternal peace), 1795.

[100] "Europe's farm follies", The Economist 10.12.2005.

[101] See Grotius, J.-J. Rousseau, Carl Schmitt, Leo Strauss.

[102] C. Albrecht published the interesting essay "Die Brücke Poul-Serrho. Geltungschancen universalistischer Ethik", dealing with this topic, in K. Acham (ed..): "Moral und Kunst im Zeitalter der Globalisierung".

103 This is evident from the subsidies paid to the Hans Böckler Foundation of the Federation of German Trade Unions, which according to Wikipedia has an annual budget of 40 million euros.

104 D. Landes described this very clearly: see Annex to the second essay "Legal certainty and prosperity".

105 In the space of just 30 years, the number of civil servants in France has quadrupled (Le Figaro 07.02.2005) – see also J. Ellul: "Le Système Technicien", Paris 1977, new edition 2004 and E. Balladur: "Machiavel en Démocratie – Mécanique du Pouvoir", Paris 2006.

106 Cases of democratic failure are listed in the Ordo Almanach 2005.

107 K. P. Krause: "Irrwege und Erosionen – Diverse Fälle von Demokratieversagen", FAZ 18.07.2006.

108 H. Giersch: "Egalität oder Prosperität – Über die Globalisierung als Schicksal und Aufgabe", in the Wirtschaftswoche magazine 13.03.1997.

109 See R. Dawkins, J. Diamond, I. Eibl-Eibesfeldt, K. Lorenz …

110 See Spain's social benefits law that guarantees food, clothing and housing (BOE Boletin Oficial del Estado dated 07.07.2009).

111 See FAZ dated 13.09.2006.

112 "Voici pourquoi les terroristes sont à l'aise en France", Figaro 12.02.1983 shows how these people have provided fertile ground for terrorism. See also A. Sokal: "Beyond the Hoax – Science, Philosophy and Culture", Oxford 2008 about ridiculing natural sciences.

113 Russo, p. 378 (Avicenna omits to mention architecture – see the construction of cathedrals, author's comment).

114 Russo, p. 379.

115 See Annex 6.5.

116 Western Europe had approximately 30 million inhabitants in the year 900, about 10 per cent of the global population, in other words. It took 900 years for this figure to double. Now we have more than 7 billion inhabitants and the rate of doubling is less than 40 years (Brockhaus 1978, Vol. 2, p. 95), and only 5 per cent of the world's population lives in Western Europe.

117 H. M. Enzensberger: "Schreckens Männer – Versuch über den radikalen Verlierer", Frankfurt 2006.

118 Bonnassie, pp. 157–264.

119 Bonnassie, pp. 164–165, 203, 257–259.

120 Almodis was Eleonore of Aquitaine's (1122–1204) predecessor and 3rd generation ancestor. The latter was one of the most powerful women in the Middle Ages and became Queen of both France and England. A documentary film portraying her history was produced in 1968

under the title of "The Lion in Winter", starring Oscar winner Katharine Hepburn.

[121] Almodis, Confessions d'outre temps (france3sud), 26 min.
[122] See also Jonathan I. Israel: "Radical Enlightenment – Philosophy and the Making of Modernity 1650–1750", Oxford 2001, for a critical discussion on this topic.
[123] D. Perler: "Zweifel und Gewissheit – Skeptische Debatten im Mittelalter", Frankfurt 2006.
[124] M. Reder and J. Schmidt (ed.): "Ein Bewusstsein von dem, was fehlt – Eine Diskussion mit Jürgen Habermas", Frankfurt 2008.
[125] H. Albert: "Joseph Ratzingers Rettung des Christentums – Beschränkungen des Vernunftgebrauchs im Dienste des Glaubens", Aschaffenburg 2008.
[126] H. Schnädelbach: "Der Fluch des Christentums" (The Curse of Christianity), Die Zeit 2000 and "Religion in der modernen Welt" (Religion in the Modern World), Frankfurt 2009, review by C. Geyer, Wer glauben will, zweifle, FAZ May 2009.
[127] The Ottawa Citizen dated 28.08.2006.
[128] Nobel Peace Prize 2006 awarded to Muhammad Yunus and the Grameen Bank (Pakistan).
[129] R. Lerner and M. Mahdi (ed.): "Medieval Political Philosophy", New York 1963, pp. 335–354.
[130] FAZ 05.09.2006.
[131] Source: Brockhaus 1978 Vol. 2, p. 95 (World).
[132] I found this remarkable account of the great Jewish scholar Moses Maimonides in J. Attali's book "Phares: 24 destins" (Beacons: 24 destinies), pp. 181–183. The text shows that I am not alone in my views on the origins of medieval liberalism (see my first essay). Maurice-Ruben Hayoun has written a detailed biography, which was published in Paris in 2009.
[133] British Library – Source: D. Hägermann, Technik im frühen Mittelalter zwischen 500 und 1000, in W. König (ed.): "Propyläen Technikgeschichte", Vol. 1, p. 331, Berlin 1991.

Index

Acknowledgments

Even a small book like this would not be possible without many mothers and fathers. That is why I would like to begin by thanking the initiators of the "Philosophy of Economics" course at the Open University of Hagen with special thanks to Prof. Dr. K. Röttgers, Dr. L. Immerthal and Prof. Dr. Dr. A. Brink, as well as my fellow students. Since 1999, the European Forum in Alpbach (Tirol) has given me the opportunity to meet distinguished personalities in the field of science. This has played an important role. Among them are Professors H. Albert (Critical Rationalism), C. Albrecht (The Intellectual Formation of the Federal Republic – A History of the Impact of Frankfurt School), R. E. Backhouse (Keynes and Hayek), Nobel Prize winner J. M. Buchanan (Institutions), J. L. Casti (Complexity), H. F. Cohen (Historiography), J. Dunn (Democracy), M. Esfeld (Causes/Reasons), V. Gadenne (Philosophy of Science), T. E. Huff (Early Modern Science), A. Musgrave (Rationalism), V. Vanberg (Free Market Economy) and W. Vosskamp (Utopias). The seminar on "The Rise of Scientific Europe" at the Open University, which was accompanied by Dr. Marie Addyman, was also paramount.

I owe a special thanks to my friends Dr. Peter and Renate Günther, Dr. Klaus and Elke Schulz-Hanssen, Dr. Hannes and Sibylle Frank (with whom my wife and I traveled the world), Rüdiger Meyer, Werner Rösch, Dr. Karl and Ursula Müller, Dr. Ergin and Karin Algim, Prof. Jean Bonamour, Volker Heimann, Dr. Gernot and Charlotte Litzenburger, Manuel Arqués, Dr. Jim Dikeou, Tony Murray, Dr. Andrej and Ljuba Zajc, Prof. Heinz Klopfer, Prof. Rainer Sasse with whom many a topic was discussed and who always showed great patience. Of course, they do not agree with me on every topic: how could they when even the experts are unable to come to a consensus – not even in Habermas' utopian dialog? Yet, I truly hope their resistance has improved my arguments. My daughter Ines Seidler-Gruber, a graduate engineer, followed the birth of this work with great interest and made numerous suggestions. Had it not been for the dedication shown by Annika Ollmann at BoD publishing house, an anonymous editor and the translator, I would have been forced to forgo the publishing of this book. I would like to take this opportunity to express my extreme gratitude for their help.

Last but not least, I would like to express my heartfelt appreciation to my wife Christa, to whom this book is dedicated, for her crucial support, engaging in daily discussions throughout the creation of these essays and her deep understanding of all of the difficulties that arose during this project in addition to the 'everyday' problems of a mid-sized business.